P9-AGV-216

LIGHT Cooking

Publications International, Ltd.
Favorite Brand Name Recipes at www.fbnr.com

Louis Weber, CEO
Publications International, Ltd.
7373 North Cicero Avenue
Lincolnwood, IL 60712

Some of the products listed in this publication may be in limited distribution.

Pictured on the front cover: Lemon Raspberry Tiramisu *(page 360).*

Pictured on the back cover *(clockwise from top):* Hawaiian Shrimp Kabobs *(page 156),* Sensational Spinach Salad with Orange Poppy Seed Vinaigrette *(page 250)* and Oatmeal Date Cookies *(page 332).*

ISBN: 0-7853-5254-6

Library of Congress Control Number: 2001093817

Manufactured in China.

8 7 6 5 4 3 2 1

Nutritional Analysis: The nutritional information that appears with each recipe was submitted in part by the participating companies and associations. Every effort has been made to check the accuracy of these numbers. However, because numerous variables account for a wide range of values for certain foods, nutritive analyses in this book should be considered approximate.

Microwave Cooking: Microwave ovens vary in wattage. Use the cooking times as guidelines and check for doneness before adding more time.

Preparation/Cooking Times: Preparation times are based on the approximate amount of time required to assemble the recipe before cooking, baking, chilling or serving. These times include preparation steps such as measuring, chopping and mixing. The fact that some preparations and cooking can be done simultaneously is taken into account. Preparation of optional ingredients and serving suggestions is not included.

Contents

Enjoy Food for Life!

Think "Good"

Eating is one of life's greatest pleasures. What better feeling is there than the one you get when you sink your teeth into a bite of dark, rich, chocolate-fudge cake or into a thick and juicy grilled-to-perfection burger? Your taste buds tingle. Your whole body feels contentment. And yet all we do is try to keep ourselves from these "bad" foods—whether we're trying to lose weight or just wanting to stay healthy. It's hard to withstand the urge for these pleasures, though. We eat the cake. We feel guilty. We eat more cake. We feel even guiltier. We need to change the way we think about food. There *are* no "bad" foods. All edible foods can be included in a healthy meal plan. The key is *moderation*.

Out with Fads

Fad diets come and go. Somehow, though, we always tend to gravitate towards what best fuels our bodies' needs— an appropriate combination of carbohydrates, protein and fat. Excluding any one of these nutrients puts us at risk for not getting all the vitamins, minerals and other food components our bodies need to stay healthy. Researchers are still not entirely sure of the long-term ill effects some of these fad diets might have on our bodies. By including all nutrients in our meal plans and eating a wide variety of foods, we're more apt to stick to our goals and improve our chances of staying nutritionally healthy.

Choose Wisely

Fat tends to be the most talked-about nutrient when it comes to weight loss. Total calories consumed, though, should be our primary focus. The only way a person can lose weight is to take in fewer calories than he or she uses. Since fat is made up of more calories than the other nutrients, decreasing the amount of fat in our diets seems to be the easiest way to quickly cut calories. Some fat is necessary for good health, but we need to be aware of the types of fats we're consuming. Saturated fats, found most often in foods of animal origin, are the most unhealthy of the fats and should be eaten in limited amounts. Other fats, such as the ones found in fish and whole grains, have been shown to have health-protective benefits. Researchers suggest we consume these types of fats on a regular basis.

Bulk Up

Gone are the days when we equated fiber solely with the wrinkly, deep-purple natural laxative, prunes. Today we're realizing all the added cancer-preventive and heart-protective benefits of a diet filled with fiber. Healthy adults should consume between 25 and 35 grams of fiber each day. Fiber comes from a plethora of plant-based foods—fruits, vegetables,whole grains. An added benefit of fiber is its ability to give a feeling of fullness. And if you feel full, chances are better you won't eat too many extra calories. Just make sure you're drinking enough water if you start adding fiber to your diet. This will keep things moving in your system and prevent them from "binding you up."

Drink Up

Water, a necessity for life, plays an instrumental role in any healthy living plan. Healthy adults should consume between eight and ten 8-ounce cups of water a day. This amount should increase if you're taking part in any heavy physical activity and during extremely hot weather. Water is the quickest fix for a hungry belly, too. It's an easy and healthy way to fill up without a bunch of extra calories. And many times when you think you're hungry, you're actually just mildly dehydrated. So instead of going straight for that gooey chocolate brownie, first fill up on a tall glass of icy cold water and rehydrate!

Hold the Salt

The American Heart Association recommends healthy adults consume no greater than 2400 milligrams of sodium per day. While many people go through life unaffected by sodium, a great many of us have to think about it on a daily basis. Low-sodium versions of well-known foods are constantly being introduced into today's marketplace. The increased use of herbs and spices is largely a result of the heightened emphasis on lower sodium intakes for healthier living.

Plan It

Nutritional analyses are included with each recipe. Use the information as a guide in helping you plan a day full of healthy eating. While the vast majority of recipes have a lower fat content and are not extremely high in calories, you'll find a few recipes with higher amounts. Once again, moderation is the key. Any food can be part of a healthy meal plan. Just fit other foods around it.

See the Professionals

Regular checkups with your doctor are important for maintaining your current weight and health. Your blood pressure, cholesterol, blood glucose, weight and height will likely all be measured. Be especially sure to visit your doctor before embarking upon any weight-loss or exercise program. Your doctor will probably want to check your physical status before you begin. This is also a great way to get baseline numbers to measure your performance in later months. Your doctor will be able to refer you to a registered dietitian, too. This person will help design a meal plan that works best for you.

Moderation Is Key

Nutrition is a very young field. Researchers are making new discoveries nearly every day. More benefits of phytochemicals, or cancer-preventive substances in foods, are being discovered regularly. Keep an open mind and be flexible to new information. Until we know *everything* there is to know about nutrition, your best bet is to eat a variety of foods in moderation and not exclude any particular food group. Most importantly, remember no food is "bad food." So go ahead and enjoy a luscious piece of cheesecake…just plan your other foods around it.

Veggie Quesadilla Appetizers

- 2 cups Zesty Pico de Gallo (page 40)
- 10 (8-inch) flour tortillas
- 1 cup finely chopped broccoli
- 1 cup thinly sliced small mushrooms
- ¾ cup shredded carrots
- ¼ cup chopped green onions
- 1¼ cups (5 ounces) reduced-fat sharp Cheddar cheese

1. Prepare Zesty Pico de Gallo.

2. Brush both sides of tortillas lightly with water. Heat small nonstick skillet over medium heat until hot. Heat tortillas, one at a time, 30 seconds on each side. Divide vegetables among 5 tortillas; sprinkle evenly with cheese. Top with remaining 5 tortillas.

3. Cook quesadillas, one at a time, in large nonstick skillet or griddle over medium heat 2 minutes on each side or until surface is crisp and cheese is melted.

4. Cut each tortilla into 4 wedges. Serve with Zesty Pico de Gallo. Garnish as desired. *makes 20 servings*

NUTRIENTS PER SERVING

1 wedge = 1 serving

Calories:	79	Carbohydrate:	12g
Calories from Fat:	21%	Fiber:	1g
Total Fat:	2g	Protein:	4g
Saturated Fat:	1g	Sodium:	223mg
Cholesterol:	4mg		

Dietary Exchanges: 1 Starch

Tortellini Teasers

Zesty Tomato Sauce (recipe follows)
½ (9-ounce) package refrigerated cheese tortellini
1 large red or green bell pepper, cut into 1-inch pieces
2 medium carrots, peeled and sliced into ½-inch-thick pieces
1 medium zucchini, sliced into ½-inch-thick pieces
12 medium fresh mushrooms
12 cherry tomatoes

1. Prepare Zesty Tomato Sauce; keep warm.

2. Cook tortellini according to package directions; drain.

3. Alternate tortellini and vegetable pieces on long frilled wooden picks or wooden skewers. Serve as dippers with tomato sauce. *makes 6 servings*

Zesty Tomato Sauce

1 can (15 ounces) tomato purée
2 tablespoons finely chopped onion
2 tablespoons chopped fresh parsley
1 teaspoon dried oregano leaves
¼ teaspoon dried thyme leaves
¼ teaspoon salt
⅛ teaspoon black pepper

Combine tomato purée, onion, parsley, oregano and thyme in small saucepan. Heat thoroughly, stirring occasionally. Stir in salt and pepper. Garnish with carrot curl, if desired.

NUTRIENTS PER SERVING
2 kabobs = 1 serving

Calories:	136	Carbohydrate:	26g
Calories from Fat:	13%	Fiber:	4g
Total Fat:	2g	Protein:	6g
Saturated Fat:	1g	Sodium:	448mg
Cholesterol:	9mg		

Dietary Exchanges: ½ Starch, 3 Vegetable, ½ Fat

little
LANGUAGE
Which word
does not rhyme?

Chicken Quesadillas

Salsa (recipe follows)
8 ounces boneless skinless chicken breast
Nonstick cooking spray
8 corn tortillas
3 ounces soft goat cheese
4 green onions, thinly sliced
4 tablespoons canned diced green chilies
2 tablespoons chopped fresh cilantro
¾ cup (3 ounces) shredded fat-free Monterey Jack cheese

1. Prepare Salsa.

2. Cut chicken breast into very thin strips. Spray medium nonstick skillet with cooking spray; heat over medium-high heat. Add chicken; cook without stirring 2 minutes or until golden. Turn chicken; cook 2 minutes more or until no longer pink in center. Remove chicken; keep warm. Wipe skillet clean.

3. Place 2 cups water in medium bowl. Dip 1 tortilla at a time in water, then place in skillet. Cook 5 to 10 seconds on each side or until tortilla is limp. Place 4 warm tortillas in single layer on work surface; stack remaining 4 to use later.

4. Crumble equal amount of goat cheese on each of 4 tortillas; spread to within ½ inch of edge. Top with chicken, green onions, chilies, cilantro and Monterey Jack cheese. (Filling ingredients should be layered evenly.) Place remaining 4 tortillas over filling; gently press down.

5. Preheat oven to 200°F. Spray same skillet lightly with cooking spray; heat over medium-high heat. Place 1 quesadilla in skillet; cook 1 minute on each side or until crisp. Remove; keep warm in oven. Repeat with remaining quesadillas. Cut each quesadilla into 4 wedges and place on plate. Spoon salsa in center. *makes 4 servings*

Salsa

2 medium tomatoes, diced
1 green onion, minced
3 tablespoons chopped fresh cilantro
2 tablespoons lime juice
1 jalapeño pepper,* stemmed, seeded and minced

**Jalapeño peppers can sting and irritate the skin; wear rubber gloves when handling peppers and do not touch eyes. Wash hands after handling.*

Combine all ingredients in medium bowl.

NUTRIENTS PER SERVING

1 quesadilla (4 wedges) = 1 serving

Calories:	290	Carbohydrate:	29g
Calories from Fat:	23%	Fiber:	2g
Total Fat:	7g	Protein:	26g
Saturated Fat:	4g	Sodium:	432mg
Cholesterol:	44mg		

Dietary Exchanges: 1½ Starch, 1 Vegetable, 3 Lean Meat

Pimiento Cheese Toast

- 1 unsliced loaf French bread
- 1 cup (4 ounces) shredded reduced-fat sharp Cheddar cheese
- 2 tablespoons diced pimiento
- 2 tablespoons reduced-fat mayonnaise
- 1 teaspoon lemon juice
- ¼ teaspoon dried oregano leaves

1. Slice bread into eight 1-inch-thick slices. Toast lightly in toaster or toaster oven.

2. Combine cheese and pimiento in medium bowl. Stir mayonnaise, lemon juice and oregano together in small bowl; add to cheese mixture. Spread 1 tablespoon mixture onto each slice of toast.

3. Preheat broiler. Place prepared toast on broiler rack. Broil 4 inches from heat 2 minutes. Serve immediately.

makes 8 servings

NUTRIENTS PER SERVING

1 slice = 1 serving

Calories:	203	Carbohydrate:	31g
Calories from Fat:	21%	Fiber:	0g
Total Fat:	5g	Protein:	8g
Saturated Fat:	1g	Sodium:	541mg
Cholesterol:	9mg		

Dietary Exchanges: 2 Starch, ½ Lean Meat, ½ Fat

Apple, Goat Cheese & Prosciutto Bruschetta

¼ cup goat cheese, softened at room temperature
¾ teaspoon minced fresh thyme, *or* ¼ teaspoon dried thyme leaves
¼ teaspoon freshly ground black pepper
8 slices (or half slices) firm, crusty bread, about 3×4 inches each
8 thin slices prosciutto, about ¼ pound
1 Fuji apple, cored and very thinly sliced

1. Preheat broiler. Combine cheese, thyme and black pepper; set aside. Place bread on baking sheet; broil, about 6 inches from heat, until lightly toasted. Loosely pleat prosciutto onto bread. Cut each piece of bread in half and arrange apple slices, then cheese mixture, over prosciutto.

2. Place bruschetta on baking sheet. Broil until cheese softens slightly. Serve as a first course or pass as an hors d'oeuvre. *makes 16 pieces (4 servings)*

Favorite recipe from **Washington Apple Commission**

NUTRIENTS PER SERVING
4 pieces = 1 serving

Calories:	275	Carbohydrate:	37g
Calories from Fat:	27%	Fiber:	3g
Total Fat:	8g	Protein:	15g
Saturated Fat:	2g	Sodium:	917mg
Cholesterol:	29mg		

Dietary Exchanges: 2 Starch, ½ Fruit, 1 Lean Meat, 1 Fat

Tip

Prosciutto means "ham" in Italian. You can find it in Italian markets, gourmet stores and some supermarkets. Prosciutto should look moist and golden-pink in color. It is often sliced transparently thin.

Creamy Dill Veggie Dip

- 4 ounces reduced-fat cream cheese
- 2 tablespoons fat-free (skim) milk
- ½ package dry ranch salad dressing mix (about 2 tablespoons)
- 1½ teaspoons dried dill weed *or* 1 tablespoon fresh dill
- 4 cups raw vegetables (such as cherry tomatoes, celery sticks, baby carrots, broccoli florets, cucumber slices, zucchini slices and/or red or green bell pepper strips)
- 8 unsalted bread sticks

Place cream cheese, milk, dressing mix and dill weed in blender container; cover and blend until smooth. Store, tightly sealed, in refrigerator.

Serve dip with vegetables and bread sticks.

makes 8 servings

NUTRIENTS PER SERVING

2 tablespoons dip plus ½ cup vegetables and 1 bread stick = 1 serving

Calories:	90	Carbohydrate:	12g
Calories from Fat:	33%	Fiber:	1g
Total Fat:	3g	Protein:	4g
Saturated Fat:	2g	Sodium:	239mg
Cholesterol:	7mg		

Dietary Exchanges: ¾ Starch, 1 Vegetable, ½ Fat

Tip

This is a great low-fat snack to have on hand. Reach for it when you're looking for something to hold you over between meals.

Mini Marinated Beef Skewers

- 1 pound lean beef round tip, cut 1 inch thick
- 2 tablespoons low-sodium soy sauce
- 1 tablespoon dry sherry
- 1 teaspoon dark sesame oil
- 2 cloves garlic, minced
- 18 cherry tomatoes (optional)

1. Cut beef across the grain into ⅛-inch slices. Place in large resealable plastic food storage bag. Combine soy sauce, sherry, oil and garlic in cup; pour over steak. Seal bag; turn to coat. Marinate in refrigerator at least 30 minutes or up to 2 hours.

2. Soak 18 (6-inch) skewers 20 minutes in water to cover.

3. Drain steak; discard marinade. Weave beef accordion-fashion onto skewers. Place on rack of broiler pan.

4. Broil 4 to 5 inches from heat 2 minutes. Turn skewers over; broil 2 minutes or until beef is barely pink.

5. Garnish each skewer with 1 cherry tomato, if desired. Place skewers on lettuce-lined platter. Serve warm or at room temperature.

makes 6 servings

NUTRIENTS PER SERVING

3 skewers = 1 serving

Calories:	120	Carbohydrate:	2g
Calories from Fat:	30%	Fiber:	<1g
Total Fat:	4g	Protein:	20g
Saturated Fat:	1g	Sodium:	99mg
Cholesterol:	60mg		

Dietary Exchanges: 2 Lean Meat

Buffalo Chicken Tenders

- 3 tablespoons Louisiana-style hot sauce
- ½ teaspoon paprika
- ¼ teaspoon ground red pepper
- 1 pound chicken tenders
- ½ cup fat-free blue cheese dressing
- ¼ cup reduced-fat sour cream
- 2 tablespoons crumbled blue cheese
- 1 medium red bell pepper, cut into ½-inch slices

1. Preheat oven to 375°F. Combine hot sauce, paprika and ground red pepper in small bowl; brush on all surfaces of chicken. Place chicken in greased 11×7-inch baking pan. Cover; marinate in refrigerator 30 minutes.

2. Bake, uncovered, about 15 minutes or until chicken is no longer pink in center.

3. Combine blue cheese dressing, sour cream and blue cheese in small serving bowl. Serve with chicken and bell pepper for dipping. *makes 10 servings*

NUTRIENTS PER SERVING

Calories:	83	Carbohydrate:	5g
Calories from Fat:	27%	Fiber:	0g
Total Fat:	2g	Protein:	9g
Saturated Fat:	1g	Sodium:	180mg
Cholesterol:	27mg		

Dietary Exchanges: ½ Starch, 1 Lean Meat

Tip

A bar in Buffalo, New York, was the first to serve deep-fried chicken wings coated in a spicy hot sauce, with blue cheese dressing for dipping. Chicken served this way has since been called "buffalo chicken" or "buffalo wings."

Crabmeat Crostini

- 1 pound Florida blue crab or stone crab meat
- 1½ cups shredded low-fat mozzarella cheese
- ½ cup Florida pecan pieces, toasted and chopped
- 2 Florida datil peppers, seeded and chopped (or other hot peppers)
- 2 teaspoons chopped fresh Florida rosemary leaves
- 2 teaspoons chopped fresh Florida thyme leaves
- 1 (3-ounce) package red dried tomatoes, rehydrated and chopped
- 12 (1-inch-thick) slices French bread, sliced diagonally

Remove any remaining shell particles from crab meat. Combine all ingredients except bread, mix well, cover and refrigerate for one hour. Arrange bread slices on baking sheet and place equal portions of crab mixture on each slice. Broil 4 to 6 inches from source of heat for 6 to 8 minutes or until cheese melts or begins to brown.

makes 12 appetizer servings

Favorite recipe from **Florida Department of Agriculture and Consumer Services, Bureau of Seafood and Aquaculture**

NUTRIENTS PER SERVING

1 slice = 1 serving

Calories:	202	Carbohydrate:	20g
Calories from Fat:	33%	Fiber:	2g
Total Fat:	7g	Protein:	15g
Saturated Fat:	2g	Sodium:	516mg
Cholesterol:	40mg		

Dietary Exchanges: 1 Starch, 2 Lean Meat, ½ Fat

Datil peppers are golden-colored, somewhat elongated and wrinkly. They resemble dates that have not yet been harvested. In fact, "datil" means "date" in Catalan Spanish. Substitute habanero peppers or Scotch bonnet peppers if you can't find datils.

Pinwheel Appetizers

- 3 cups cooked wild rice
- 1 package (8 ounces) nonfat pasteurized process cream cheese product
- ⅓ cup grated Parmesan cheese
- 1 teaspoon dried parsley flakes
- ½ teaspoon garlic powder
- ½ teaspoon Dijon-style mustard
- 2 to 3 drops hot pepper sauce (optional)
- 3 (12-inch) soft flour tortillas
- 2½ ounces thinly sliced corned beef
- 9 fresh spinach leaves

Combine wild rice, cream cheese, Parmesan cheese, parsley, garlic powder, mustard and pepper sauce, if desired. Spread evenly over tortillas, leaving ½-inch border on one side of each tortilla. Place single layer corned beef over rice and cheese mixture. Top with layer of spinach. Roll each tortilla tightly toward ½-inch border. Moisten border of tortilla with water; press to seal roll. Wrap tightly in plastic wrap. Refrigerate several hours or overnight. Cut into 1-inch slices. *makes 36 appetizers*

Favorite recipe from **Minnesota Cultivated Wild Rice Council**

NUTRIENTS PER SERVING

Calories:	37	Carbohydrate:	5g
Calories from Fat:	21%	Fiber:	<1g
Total Fat:	1g	Protein:	2g
Saturated Fat:	<1g	Sodium:	91mg
Cholesterol:	4mg		

Dietary Exchanges: ½ Starch

Oriental Salsa

- 1 cup diced, unpeeled cucumber
- ½ cup chopped red bell pepper
- ½ cup thinly sliced green onions
- ⅓ cup coarsely chopped fresh cilantro
- 1 clove garlic, minced
- 2 tablespoons low-sodium soy sauce
- 1 tablespoon rice vinegar
- ½ teaspoon dark sesame oil
- ¼ teaspoon red pepper flakes
- Easy Wonton Chips (recipe follows) or assorted fresh vegetables for dipping

Combine all ingredients except Easy Wonton Chips in medium bowl until well blended. Cover; refrigerate until serving time. Serve with Easy Wonton Chips or assorted fresh vegetables for dipping. Or, use as an accompaniment to broiled fish, chicken or pork. *makes 4 servings*

Easy Wonton Chips

- 1 tablespoon low-sodium soy sauce
- 2 teaspoons peanut or vegetable oil
- ½ teaspoon sugar
- ¼ teaspoon garlic salt
- 12 wonton wrappers

1. Preheat oven to 375°F. Combine soy sauce, oil, sugar and garlic salt in small bowl; mix well.

2. Cut each wonton wrapper diagonally in half. Place on 15×10-inch jelly-roll pan coated with nonstick cooking spray. Brush soy mixture lightly but evenly over both sides of skins.

3. Bake 4 to 6 minutes or until crisp and lightly browned, turning after 3 minutes. Transfer to cooling rack; cool completely. *makes 2 dozen chips*

NUTRIENTS PER SERVING

Calories:	116	Carbohydrate:	17g
Calories from Fat:	25%	Fiber:	1g
Total Fat:	3g	Protein:	4g
Saturated Fat:	<1g	Sodium:	723mg
Cholesterol:	2mg		

Dietary Exchanges: ½ Starch, ½ Vegetable, ½ Fat

Oriental Salsa with Easy Wonton Chips

Caponata Spread

- 1½ tablespoons olive or vegetable oil
- 1 medium eggplant, diced (about 4 cups)
- 1 medium onion, chopped
- 1½ cups water
- 1 envelope LIPTON® RECIPE SECRETS® Savory Herb with Garlic Soup Mix
- 2 tablespoons chopped fresh parsley (optional)
- Salt and ground black pepper to taste
- Pita chips or thinly sliced Italian or French bread

In 10-inch nonstick skillet, heat oil over medium heat and cook eggplant with onion 3 minutes. Add ½ cup water. Reduce heat to low and simmer covered 3 minutes. Stir in Savory Herb with Garlic Soup Mix blended with remaining 1 cup water. Bring to a boil over high heat. Reduce heat to low and simmer uncovered, stirring occasionally, 20 minutes. Stir in parsley, salt and pepper. Serve with pita chips. *makes about 4 cups spread*

NUTRIENTS PER SERVING

2 tablespoons spread= 1 serving

Calories:	13	Carbohydrate:	2g
Calories from Fat:	43%	Fiber:	<1g
Total Fat:	1g	Protein:	<1g
Saturated Fat:	<1g	Sodium:	60mg
Cholesterol:	0mg		

Dietary Exchanges: Free

Hummus

- 1 can (about 15 ounces) garbanzo beans (chick-peas), rinsed and drained
- 3 tablespoons lemon juice
- 4½ teaspoons tahini*
- ½ teaspoon ground cumin
- ¼ teaspoon salt
- ¼ teaspoon black pepper
- ½ cup chopped seeded tomato
- ⅓ cup chopped red onion
- ⅓ cup chopped celery
- ⅓ cup chopped seeded cucumber
- ⅓ cup chopped green or red bell pepper
- 2 pita loaves

***Tahini, a thick paste made from ground sesame seeds, is available in the ethnic section of major supermarkets, Middle Eastern markets or health food stores.**

1. Combine beans, lemon juice, tahini, cumin, salt and black pepper in work bowl of food processor or blender container; process until smooth. If mixture is too thick to spread, add water until desired consistency is reached.

2. Spoon bean mixture into serving bowl. Top with tomato, onion, celery, cucumber and bell pepper.

3. Preheat broiler. Split pita loaves open to form 4 rounds. Stack rounds; cut into sixths to form 24 wedges. Place wedges on baking sheet. Broil 3 minutes or until crisp.

4. Serve Hummus with warm pita bread wedges.

makes 6 servings

NUTRIENTS PER SERVING

4 wedges = 1 serving

Calories:	188	Carbohydrate:	33g
Calories from Fat:	17%	Fiber:	4g
Total Fat:	4g	Protein:	7g
Saturated Fat:	1g	Sodium:	542mg
Cholesterol:	0mg		

Dietary Exchanges: 2 Starch, ½ Vegetable, ½ Fat

Spicy Vegetable Quesadillas

Nonstick cooking spray
1 small zucchini, chopped
½ cup chopped green bell pepper
½ cup chopped onion
2 cloves garlic, minced
½ teaspoon chili powder
½ teaspoon ground cumin
8 (6-inch) flour tortillas
1 cup (4 ounces) shredded reduced-fat Cheddar cheese
¼ cup chopped fresh cilantro

1. Spray large nonstick skillet with cooking spray. Heat over medium heat until hot. Add zucchini, bell pepper, onion, garlic, chili powder and cumin; cook and stir 3 to 4 minutes or until vegetables are crisp-tender. Remove vegetables and set aside; wipe skillet clean.

2. Spoon vegetable mixture evenly over half of each tortilla. Sprinkle each evenly with cheese and cilantro. Fold each tortilla in half.

3. Spray same skillet with cooking spray. Add tortillas and heat over medium heat 1 to 2 minutes per side or until lightly browned. Cut into thirds before serving.

makes 8 servings

NUTRIENTS PER SERVING

1 quesadilla (3 wedges) = 1 serving

Calories:	153	Carbohydrate:	23g
Calories from Fat:	22%	Fiber:	1g
Total Fat:	4g	Protein:	7g
Saturated Fat:	1g	Sodium:	201mg
Cholesterol:	8mg		

Dietary Exchanges: 1½ Starch, 1 Lean Meat

Spinach-Stuffed Appetizer Shells

18 jumbo pasta shells (about 6 ounces)
1 package (10 ounces) frozen chopped spinach, thawed and well drained
1 can (8 ounces) water chestnuts, drained and chopped
¾ cup nonfat ricotta cheese
½ cup reduced-fat mayonnaise
¼ cup finely chopped carrot
3 tablespoons finely chopped onion
¾ teaspoon garlic powder
¾ teaspoon hot pepper sauce

1. Cook shells according to package directions, omitting salt. Rinse under cold running water until shells are cool; drain well.

2. Combine remaining ingredients in medium bowl; mix well.

3. Fill each shell with about 3 tablespoons spinach mixture; cover. Refrigerate up to 12 hours before serving. Garnish, if desired. *makes 9 servings*

NUTRIENTS PER SERVING

2 stuffed shells = 1 serving

Calories:	155	Carbohydrate:	21g
Calories from Fat:	29%	Fiber:	3g
Total Fat:	5g	Protein:	6g
Saturated Fat:	1g	Sodium:	172mg
Cholesterol:	2mg		

Dietary Exchanges: 1 Starch, 1 Vegetable, 1 Fat

recipe tip

Replace the mayonnaise in this recipe with fat-free mayonnaise, and you'll be cutting even more calories and fat!

Cheesy Potato Skin Appetizers

⅔ cup Zesty Pico de Gallo (page 40) or purchased salsa
5 potatoes (4 to 5 ounces each)
Nonstick butter-flavor cooking spray
4 ounces fat-free cream cheese
2 tablespoons reduced-fat sour cream
⅓ cup shredded reduced-fat sharp Cheddar cheese
2 tablespoons sliced ripe olives (optional)
¼ cup minced fresh cilantro

1. Prepare Zesty Pico de Gallo.

2. Preheat oven to 425°F. Scrub potatoes; pierce several times with fork. Bake 45 minutes or until soft. Cool.

3. Split each potato lengthwise into halves. Scoop out potato with spoon, leaving ¼-inch shell. (Reserve potato for another use.) Place potato skins on baking sheet; spray lightly with cooking spray.

4. Preheat broiler. Broil potato skins 6 inches from heat 5 minutes or until lightly brown and crisp.

5. *Reduce oven temperature to 350°F.* Combine cream cheese and sour cream; stir until well blended. Divide among potato skins; spread to cover. Top with Zesty Pico de Gallo, cheese and olives, if desired. Bake 15 minutes or until heated through. Sprinkle with cilantro.

makes 10 servings

continued on page 40

Cheesy Potato Skin Appetizers with Zesty Pico de Gallo (page 40)

Cheesy Potato Skin Appetizers, continued

Zesty Pico de Gallo

2 cups chopped seeded tomatoes
1 cup chopped green onions
1 can (8 ounces) tomato sauce
½ cup minced fresh cilantro
1 to 2 tablespoons minced jalapeño peppers*
1 tablespoon fresh lime juice

**Jalapeño peppers can sting and irritate the skin; wear rubber gloves when handling peppers and do not touch eyes. Wash hands after handling.*

Combine all ingredients in medium bowl. Cover and refrigerate at least 1 hour. *makes 4 cups (20 servings)*

NUTRIENTS PER SERVING

1 potato skin appetizer
plus about 3½ tablespoons pico de gallo = 1 serving

Calories:	86	Carbohydrate:	15g
Calories from Fat:	10%	Fiber:	3g
Total Fat:	1g	Protein:	4g
Saturated Fat:	1g	Sodium:	149mg
Cholesterol:	4mg		

Dietary Exchanges: 1 Starch

Savory Sweet Potato Sticks

3 medium sweet potatoes (about 1½ pounds)
3 cups KELLOGG'S® RICE KRISPIES® cereal, crushed to ¾ cup
½ teaspoon garlic salt
¼ teaspoon onion salt
⅛ teaspoon cayenne
½ cup all-purpose flour
2 egg whites
2 tablespoons water
Salsa (optional)

1. Wash potatoes and cut lengthwise into ½-inch slices. Cut slices into ½-inch strips. Set aside.

2. In shallow pan or plate, combine Kellogg's® Rice Krispies® cereal and spices. Set aside. Place flour in second shallow pan or plate. Set aside. Beat together egg whites and water. Set aside. Coat potatoes with flour, shaking off excess. Dip coated potatoes in egg mixture, then coat with cereal mixture. Place in single layer on foil-lined baking sheet coated with cooking spray.

3. Bake at 400°F about 30 minutes or until lightly browned. Serve hot with salsa, if desired.

makes 15 servings

Prep Time: 25 minutes
Bake Time: 15 minutes

NUTRIENTS PER SERVING

Calories: 82
Calories from Fat: ..1%
Total Fat: ....<1g
Saturated Fat: .....<1g
Cholesterol: 0mg
Carbohydrate: 18g
Fiber: 2g
Protein: 2g
Sodium: 166mg

Dietary Exchanges: 1 Starch

Pizza Breadsticks

- 1 package (¼ ounce) active dry yeast
- ¾ cup warm water (105° to 115°F)
- 2½ cups all-purpose flour
- ½ cup (2 ounces) shredded part-skim mozzarella cheese
- ¼ cup (1 ounce) shredded Parmesan cheese
- ¼ cup chopped red bell pepper
- 1 green onion with top, sliced
- 1 medium clove garlic, minced
- ½ teaspoon dried basil leaves, crushed
- ½ teaspoon dried oregano leaves, crushed
- ¼ teaspoon red pepper flakes (optional)
- ¼ teaspoon salt
- 1 tablespoon olive oil

1. Preheat oven to 400°F. Spray 2 large nonstick baking sheets with nonstick cooking spray; set aside.

2. Sprinkle yeast over warm water in small bowl; stir until yeast dissolves. Let stand 5 minutes or until bubbly.

3. Meanwhile, place all remaining ingredients except olive oil in food processor; process a few seconds to combine. With food processor running, gradually add yeast mixture and olive oil. Process just until mixture forms a ball. (Add an additional 2 tablespoons flour if dough is too sticky.)

4. Transfer dough to lightly floured surface; knead 1 minute. Let dough rest 5 minutes. Roll out dough with lightly floured rolling pin to form 14×8-inch rectangle; cut dough crosswise into ½-inch-wide strips. Twist dough strips; place on prepared baking sheets.

5. Bake 14 to 16 minutes or until lightly browned.

makes 14 servings

NUTRIENTS PER SERVING

2 breadsticks = 1 serving

Calories:	112	Carbohydrate:	18g
Calories from Fat:	19%	Fiber:	1g
Total Fat:	2g	Protein:	4g
Saturated Fat:	1g	Sodium:	91mg
Cholesterol:	4mg		

Dietary Exchanges: 1 Starch, ½ Fat

Greek Isles Omelet

Nonstick cooking spray
¼ cup chopped onion
¼ cup canned artichoke hearts, rinsed and drained
¼ cup washed and torn spinach leaves
¼ cup chopped plum tomato
1 cup cholesterol-free egg substitute
2 tablespoons sliced pitted ripe olives, rinsed and drained
Dash black pepper

1. Spray small nonstick skillet with cooking spray; heat over medium heat until hot. Cook and stir onion 2 minutes or until crisp-tender.

2. Add artichoke hearts. Cook and stir until heated through. Add spinach and tomato; toss briefly. Remove from heat. Transfer vegetables to small bowl. Wipe out skillet and spray with cooking spray.

3. Combine egg substitute, olives and pepper in medium bowl. Heat skillet over medium heat until hot. Pour egg mixture into skillet. Cook over medium heat 5 to 7 minutes; as eggs begin to set, gently lift edges of omelet with spatula and tilt skillet so that uncooked portion flows underneath.

4. When egg mixture is set, spoon vegetable mixture over half of omelet. Loosen omelet with spatula and fold in half. Slide omelet onto serving plate. Garnish as desired.

makes 2 servings

NUTRIENTS PER SERVING

Calories:	111	Carbohydrate:	7g
Calories from Fat:	26%	Fiber:	1g
Total Fat:	3g	Protein:	13g
Saturated Fat:	<1g	Sodium:	538mg
Cholesterol:	0mg		

Dietary Exchanges: 1 Vegetable, 2 Lean Meat

Blueberry-Bran Pancakes

- 1 cup FIBER ONE® cereal
- 2 egg whites or 1 egg, beaten slightly
- 1¼ cups buttermilk or milk
- 2 tablespoons vegetable oil
- 1 cup GOLD MEDAL® all-purpose flour
- 1 tablespoon sugar
- 1 teaspoon baking powder
- ½ teaspoon baking soda
- ½ teaspoon salt
- ½ cup fresh or frozen (thawed and well drained) blueberries

1. Spray unheated skillet or griddle with cooking spray, then heat over medium-high heat until hot (or electric griddle to 375°F).

2. Crush cereal.* Stir together egg whites, buttermilk, oil and cereal in medium bowl; let stand 7 minutes. Beat in flour, sugar, baking powder, baking soda and salt with wire whisk or fork until blended. Gently stir in blueberries.

3. Pour ¼ cup batter onto hot griddle for each pancake. (If batter is too thick, stir in additional milk, 1 tablespoon at a time, until desired consistency.)

4. Cook pancakes until puffed and full of bubbles but before bubbles break. Turn and cook other sides until golden brown.

makes 10 (5-inch) pancakes

**Place cereal in plastic bag or between sheets of waxed paper and crush with rolling pin. Or, crush in blender or food processor.*

Prep Time: 15 minutes
Cook Time: 4 minutes per batch

NUTRIENTS PER SERVING

1 pancake = 1 serving

Calories:	106	Carbohydrate:	18g
Calories from Fat:	26%	Fiber:	3g
Total Fat:	3g	Protein:	3g
Saturated Fat:	1g	Sodium:	298mg
Cholesterol:	1mg		

Dietary Exchanges: 1 Starch, 1 Fat

Banana Coffee Cake

½ cup 100% bran cereal
½ cup strong coffee
1 cup mashed ripe bananas
½ cup sugar
1 egg, slightly beaten
2 tablespoons canola or vegetable oil
½ cup all-purpose flour
½ cup whole wheat flour
2 teaspoons baking powder
1 teaspoon ground cinnamon
¼ teaspoon salt

1. Preheat oven to 350°F. Coat 8-inch square baking pan with nonstick cooking spray; set aside. Combine bran cereal and coffee in large bowl; let stand 3 minutes or until cereal softens. Stir in bananas, sugar, egg and oil.

2. Combine all-purpose flour, whole wheat flour, baking powder, cinnamon and salt in small bowl; stir into banana mixture just until moistened. Pour into prepared pan.

3. Bake 25 to 35 minutes or until wooden toothpick inserted into center of cake comes out clean. Cool in pan on wire rack. *makes 9 servings*

NUTRIENTS PER SERVING

Calories:	169	Carbohydrate:	30g
Calories from Fat:	22%	Fiber:	3g
Total Fat:	4g	Protein:	3g
Saturated Fat:	<1g	Sodium:	166mg
Cholesterol:	24mg		

Dietary Exchanges: 1 Starch, 1 Fruit, 1 Fat

recipe tip

Ripen bananas by storing them at room temperature. Speed ripening by placing them in an unsealed paper bag. Once bananas have ripened, you can keep them from spoiling by storing them, tightly wrapped, in the refrigerator. Although the peel will turn brown, the fruit will retain its creamy color for about three days.

Blueberry Lemon Scones

- 2⅔ cups all-purpose flour
- ½ cup plus 2 tablespoons sugar, divided
- 2½ teaspoons baking powder
- 1 teaspoon baking soda
- ½ teaspoon salt
- ½ cup dried blueberries
- 1 container (8 ounces) nonfat lemon yogurt
- ⅓ cup Dried Plum Purée (recipe follows) or prepared dried plum butter
- 3 tablespoons butter or margarine, melted
- 1 tablespoon grated lemon peel
- 2 teaspoons vanilla
- ¼ teaspoon ground nutmeg

Preheat oven to 400°F. Coat baking sheet with vegetable cooking spray. In large bowl, combine flour, ½ cup sugar, baking powder, baking soda and salt. Add blueberries. In small bowl, mix yogurt, dried plum purée, butter, lemon peel and vanilla until blended. Add to flour mixture; mix just until mixture holds together. Turn dough out onto lightly floured surface and pat into 10-inch round. Combine the remaining 2 tablespoons sugar and nutmeg; sprinkle evenly over dough. Pat sugar mixture gently into dough; cut into 12 equal wedges. Place wedges on prepared baking sheet, spacing 1 inch apart. Bake in center of oven about 15 minutes until lightly browned and cracked on top. Remove to wire rack to cool slightly.

makes 12 scones

variation: Substitute currants, raisins or chopped dried cherries for the blueberries.

Dried Plum Purée: Combine 1⅓ cups (8 ounces) pitted dried plums and 6 tablespoons hot water in container of food processor or blender. Pulse on and off until dried plums are finely chopped and smooth. Store leftovers in covered container in refrigerator for up to two months. Makes 1 cup.

Favorite recipe from **California Dried Plum Board**

NUTRIENTS PER SERVING

1 scone = 1 serving

Calories:	221	Carbohydrate:	44g
Calories from Fat:	14%	Fiber:	1g
Total Fat:	3g	Protein:	4g
Saturated Fat:	2g	Sodium:	351mg
Cholesterol:	8mg		

Dietary Exchanges: 2 Starch, 1 Fruit, ½ Fat

Sunrise French Toast

- 2 cups cholesterol-free egg substitute
- ½ cup evaporated skimmed milk
- 1 teaspoon grated orange peel
- 1 teaspoon vanilla
- ¼ teaspoon ground cinnamon
- 1 loaf (1 pound) Italian bread, cut into ½-inch-thick slices (about 20 slices)
- 1 jar (10 ounces) no-sugar-added orange marmalade
- Nonstick cooking spray
- Powdered sugar
- Maple-flavored syrup (optional)

1. Preheat oven to 400°F. Combine egg substitute, milk, orange peel, vanilla and cinnamon in medium bowl. Set aside.

2. Spread 1 bread slice with 1 tablespoon marmalade to within ½ inch of edge. Top with another bread slice. Repeat with remaining bread and marmalade.

3. Spray griddle or large skillet with cooking spray; heat over medium heat until hot. Dip sandwiches in egg substitute mixture. Do not soak. Cook sandwiches in batches 2 to 3 minutes on each side or until golden brown.

4. Transfer toasted sandwiches to 15×10-inch jelly-roll pan. Bake 10 to 12 minutes or until sides are sealed. Dust with powdered sugar and serve with syrup, if desired.

makes 5 servings

NUTRIENTS PER SERVING

2 sandwiches = 1 serving

Calories:	431	Carbohydrate:	82g
Calories from Fat:	7%	Fiber:	<1g
Total Fat:	4g	Protein:	16g
Saturated Fat:	1g	Sodium:	687mg
Cholesterol:	1mg		

Dietary Exchanges: 3 Starch, 2 Fruit, 1½ Lean Meat

Cranberry Cheese Crêpes

- Festive Cranberry Sauce (recipe follows)
- 1 cup all-purpose flour
- 3 tablespoons sugar, divided
- ¼ teaspoon salt
- 1 cup fat-free (skim) milk
- 1 egg
- 2 egg whites
- 1 tablespoon margarine, melted
- ¾ cup 1% low-fat cottage cheese
- 4 ounces fat-free cream cheese, softened
- 1 teaspoon vanilla
- 3 tablespoons toasted sliced almonds

1. Prepare Festive Cranberry Sauce. Combine flour, 1 tablespoon sugar and salt in medium bowl; whisk in milk, egg, egg whites and margarine until smooth.

2. Lightly grease 8-inch nonstick skillet. Heat over medium heat until hot. Remove from heat. Pour in scant ¼ cup batter; roll from side to side to cover entire skillet surface. When edges of batter curl away from side of skillet, turn crêpe over; brown. Repeat with remaining batter.

3. Place cottage cheese in food processor or blender; process until smooth. Add cream cheese, remaining 2 tablespoons sugar and vanilla; process until smooth.

4. Preheat oven to 350°F. Spoon 2 tablespoons cheese mixture into center of each crêpe. Spoon 2 tablespoons Festive Cranberry Sauce over cheese mixture. Roll crêpes up; place seam sides down on 15×10-inch jelly-roll pan. Bake 5 minutes or until heated through.

5. Place crêpes on serving plates. Spoon remaining sauce over tops; sprinkle with almonds. Garnish as desired.

makes 8 servings

Festive Cranberry Sauce

- 1 package (12 ounces) fresh or frozen cranberries, thawed
- ⅔ cup sugar
- 1 cup water, divided
- ½ teaspoon almond extract (optional)
- 2 tablespoons cornstarch

1. Combine cranberries, ⅔ cup sugar, ¾ cup water and almond extract, if desired, in medium saucepan. Bring to a boil over medium-high heat; reduce heat to low. Simmer, uncovered, 5 minutes or until cranberries are tender and sugar is dissolved completely.

continued on page 56

Cranberry Cheese Crêpe

Cranberry Cheese Crêpes, continued

2. Return mixture to a boil over medium-high heat. Stir remaining ¼ cup water into cornstarch in small cup until smooth; stir into boiling mixture. Boil 1 minute or until thickened, stirring constantly. *makes about 2½ cups*

NUTRIENTS PER SERVING

1 crêpe = 1 serving

Calories:	263	Carbohydrate:	47g
Calories from Fat:	14%	Fiber:	2g
Total Fat:	4g	Protein:	10g
Saturated Fat:	1g	Sodium:	293mg
Cholesterol:	31mg		

Dietary Exchanges: 2 Starch, 1 Fruit, ½ Lean Meat, ½ Fat

Berry and Apricot Frappé

- 2 cups orange juice
- 1 cup ice
- ½ cup frozen strawberries or raspberries
- ½ cup canned apricots in juice, drained, or fresh apricots
- ½ cup plain or flavored fat-free yogurt
- 2 tablespoons wheat germ
- 1½ teaspoons EQUAL® FOR RECIPES *or* 4½ packets EQUAL® sweetener *or* 3 tablespoons EQUAL® SPOONFUL™

• Place all ingredients in blender or food processor. Blend until smooth and all ice is crushed. *makes 2 servings*

NUTRIENTS PER SERVING

Calories:	220	Carbohydrate:	44g
Calories from Fat:	5%	Fiber:	3g
Total Fat:	1g	Protein:	10g
Saturated Fat:	<1g	Sodium:	50mg
Cholesterol:	1mg		

Dietary Exchanges: 3 Fruit, 1 Lean Meat

Rise and Shine Muffins

- 1 cup high fiber bran cereal, crushed
- ⅔ cup skim milk
- ½ cup crunchy peanut butter
- 1 cup coarsely grated apple
- ⅔ cup brown sugar
- ½ cup coarsely grated zucchini
- ½ cup coarsely grated carrots
- 1 teaspoon maple extract
- 1 egg
- 2 egg whites
- 1¾ cups whole wheat flour
- 1 tablespoon baking powder
- 1 tablespoon orange peel
- 2 teaspoons ground cinnamon
- 1 teaspoon lite salt
- Cooking spray

Preheat oven to 375°F. Mix bran cereal and milk in large bowl and let stand until softened. Fold in peanut butter, apple, brown sugar, zucchini, carrots and maple extract until mixed. In small bowl, beat egg and egg whites; fold into the bran mixture. In medium bowl, combine flour, baking powder, orange peel, cinnamon and salt. Add dry ingredients to bran mixture, but be careful not to over-mix. Spray the cups of muffin pan with cooking spray. Divide the batter evenly among muffin cups. Place shallow pan of water on bottom rack of the oven to prevent muffins from drying. Place muffins on middle rack and bake for 20 to 25 minutes until golden brown. Remove from muffin pan and serve. *makes 12 muffins*

Favorite recipe from **Peanut Advisory Board**

NUTRIENTS PER SERVING

1 muffin = 1 serving

Calories:	203	Carbohydrate:	35g
Calories from Fat:	25%	Fiber:	6g
Total Fat:	6g	Protein:	7g
Saturated Fat:	1g	Sodium:	286mg
Cholesterol:	18mg		

Dietary Exchanges: 2 Starch, 1½ Fat

Better Banana Bread

1 cup mashed very ripe bananas (about 3 small)
½ cup plain fat-free yogurt
4 tablespoons margarine, melted
1 egg
1 egg white
7¼ teaspoons EQUAL® FOR RECIPES *or* 24 packets EQUAL® sweetener *or* 1 cup EQUAL® SPOONFUL™
1 teaspoon vanilla
2 cups all-purpose flour
1 teaspoon baking powder
½ teaspoon baking soda
¼ teaspoon salt
¼ to ½ cup walnut pieces (optional)

• Beat banana, yogurt, margarine, egg, egg white, Equal® and vanilla at medium speed in large bowl until blended; beat at high speed 1 minute. Add combined flour, baking powder, baking soda and salt, mixing just until ingredients are moistened. Stir in walnuts, if desired.

• Pour batter into one 8½×4-inch greased and floured loaf pan or three 5⅝×3¼-inch loaf pans. Bake in preheated 350°F oven until bread is golden and toothpick inserted in center comes out clean, 55 to 65 minutes for large loaf, 35 to 40 minutes for small loaves. Cool 10 minutes in pan on wire rack; remove from pan and cool completely.

makes 1 loaf (8½×4 inches, 14 slices) or 3 loaves (5⅝×3¼ inches)

tip: Recipe can be doubled to make 2 large or 6 small loaves.

NUTRIENTS PER SERVING

1 of 14 slices = 1 serving

Calories:	128	Carbohydrate:	18g
Calories from Fat:	27%	Fiber:	1g
Total Fat:	4g	Protein:	5g
Saturated Fat:	1g	Sodium:	175mg
Cholesterol:	15mg		

Dietary Exchanges: 1 Starch, 1 Fat

Harvest Apple Oatmeal

1 cup apple juice
1 cup water
1 medium apple, cored and chopped
1 cup uncooked old-fashioned oats
¼ cup raisins
⅛ teaspoon salt
⅛ teaspoon ground cinnamon

MICROWAVE DIRECTIONS:

1. Combine juice, water and apple in 2-quart microwavable bowl. Microwave at HIGH 3 minutes, stirring halfway through cooking time.

2. Add oats, raisins, salt and cinnamon; stir until well blended.

3. Microwave at MEDIUM (50% power) 4 to 5 minutes or until thick; stir before serving. Garnish as desired.

makes 2 servings

conventional directions: To prepare conventionally, bring apple juice, water and apple to a boil in medium saucepan over medium-high heat. Stir in oats, raisins, salt and cinnamon until well blended. Cook uncovered, over medium heat, 5 to 6 minutes or until thick, stirring occasionally.

NUTRIENTS PER SERVING

Calories:	229	Carbohydrate:	46g
Calories from Fat:	6%	Fiber:	7g
Total Fat:	3g	Protein:	7g
Saturated Fat:	1g	Sodium:	71mg
Cholesterol:	0mg		

Dietary Exchanges: 1½ Starch, 1½ Fruit, ½ Fat

Brunch Strata

- 1 can (10¾ ounces) reduced-fat condensed cream of celery soup
- 2 cups cholesterol-free egg substitute *or* 8 eggs
- 1 cup fat-free (skim) milk
- 1 can (4 ounces) sliced mushrooms
- ¼ cup sliced green onions
- 1 teaspoon dry mustard
- ½ teaspoon salt (optional)
- ¼ teaspoon black pepper
- 6 slices reduced-fat white bread, cut into 1-inch cubes
- 4 links reduced-fat precooked breakfast sausage, thinly sliced

Preheat oven to 350°F. Combine soup, egg substitute, milk, mushrooms, onions, mustard, salt and pepper in medium bowl; mix well. Spray 2-quart baking dish with nonstick cooking spray. Combine bread, sausage and soup mixture. Bake 30 to 35 minutes or until set. *makes 6 servings*

NUTRIENTS PER SERVING

Calories:	155	Carbohydrate:	20g
Calories from Fat:	12%	Fiber:	3g
Total Fat:	2g	Protein:	15g
Saturated Fat:	1g	Sodium:	642mg
Cholesterol:	8mg		

Dietary Exchanges: 1 Starch, 2 Lean Meat

Soy Milk Smoothie

- 3 cups plain or vanilla soy milk
- 1 banana, peeled and frozen
- 1 cup frozen strawberries or raspberries
- 2½ teaspoons EQUAL® FOR RECIPES *or* 8 packets EQUAL® sweetener *or* ⅓ cup EQUAL® SPOONFUL™
- 1 teaspoon vanilla or almond extract

• Place all ingredients in blender or food processor. Blend until smooth. *makes 4 servings*

note: Peel and cut banana into large chunks. Place in plastic freezer bag; seal. Freeze at least 5 to 6 hours or overnight.

NUTRIENTS PER SERVING

Calories:	163	Carbohydrate:	24g
Calories from Fat:	22%	Fiber:	1g
Total Fat:	4g	Protein:	7g
Saturated Fat:	<1g	Sodium:	107mg
Cholesterol:	0mg		

Dietary Exchanges: 1 Fruit,1 Milk, ½ Fat

Brunch Strata

Baked Banana Doughnuts

- 2 ripe bananas, mashed
- 2 egg whites
- 1 tablespoon vegetable oil
- 1 cup packed brown sugar
- 1½ cups all-purpose flour
- ¾ cup whole wheat flour
- 2 teaspoons baking powder
- ½ teaspoon baking soda
- ¼ teaspoon pumpkin pie spice
- 1 tablespoon granulated sugar
- 2 tablespoons chopped walnuts (optional)

Preheat oven to 425°F. Spray baking sheet with nonstick cooking spray. Beat bananas, egg whites, oil and brown sugar in large bowl or food processor. Add flours, baking powder, baking soda and pumpkin pie spice. Mix until well blended. Let stand for five minutes for dough to rise. Scoop out heaping tablespoonfuls of dough onto prepared baking sheet. Using thin rubber spatula or butter knife round out doughnut hole in center of dough (if dough sticks to knife or spatula, spray with cooking spray). With spatula, smooth outside edges of dough into round doughnut shape. Repeat until all dough is used. Sprinkle with granulated sugar and walnuts, if desired. Bake 6 to 10 minutes or until tops are golden.

makes about 22 doughnuts

variation: Use 8 ounces solid pack pumpkin instead of bananas to make pumpkin doughnuts.

Favorite recipe from **The Sugar Association, Inc.**

NUTRIENTS PER SERVING

1 doughnut = 1 serving

Calories:	102	Carbohydrate:	22g
Calories from Fat:	7%	Fiber:	1g
Total Fat:	1g	Protein:	2g
Saturated Fat:	<1g	Sodium:	82mg
Cholesterol:	0mg		

Dietary Exchanges: 1 Starch, ½ Fruit

Pineapple Crunch Coffee Cake

- 1¾ cups reduced-fat baking mix
- ½ cup plus 2 tablespoons fat-free (skim) milk
- ½ cup wheat germ
- ½ cup reduced-fat sour cream
- ¼ cup granulated sugar
- 1 egg
- 1 teaspoon vanilla
- 2 cans (8 ounces each) crushed pineapple in unsweetened pineapple juice, drained
- ⅓ cup packed dark brown sugar
- ⅓ cup uncooked old-fashioned or quick oats

Preheat oven to 350°F. Coat 8-inch square baking dish with nonstick cooking spray.

Combine baking mix, milk, wheat germ, sour cream, granulated sugar, egg and vanilla in medium bowl. Stir to blend thoroughly. (Batter will be lumpy.) Spread batter in baking dish. Spoon pineapple evenly over batter. Sprinkle brown sugar and oats over pineapple.

Bake 30 minutes or until toothpick inserted into center comes out clean. Serve warm or at room temperature.

makes 9 servings

NUTRIENTS PER SERVING

Calories:	237	Carbohydrate:	44g
Calories from Fat:	14%	Fiber:	2g
Total Fat:	4g	Protein:	6g
Saturated Fat:	1g	Sodium:	267mg
Cholesterol:	28mg		

Dietary Exchanges: 2½ Starch, ½ Fruit, ½ Fat

recipe tip

After handling raw eggs, wash your hands before touching other food or equipment. Keep equipment and counter surfaces clean.

Whole Wheat Griddle Cakes with Fresh Strawberry Topping

1¼ cups whole wheat flour
1¼ cups all-purpose flour
2 tablespoons sugar
1 tablespoon baking powder
1¾ cups skim milk
1 cup EGG BEATERS® Healthy Real Egg Product
3 tablespoons FLEISCHMANN'S® Original Margarine, melted, divided
Fresh Strawberry Topping (recipe follows)

In large bowl, combine flours, sugar and baking powder. Stir in milk, Egg Beaters® and 2 tablespoons margarine just until blended. (Batter will be slightly lumpy.)

Brush large nonstick griddle or skillet with some of remaining margarine; heat over medium-high heat. Using ¼ cup batter for each pancake, pour batter onto griddle. Cook until bubbly; turn and cook until lightly browned. Repeat with remaining batter, using remaining margarine as needed, to make 16 pancakes. Serve hot with Fresh Strawberry Topping. *makes 16 (5-inch) pancakes*

Fresh Strawberry Topping: In large bowl, combine 1 quart strawberries, sliced, and ¼ cup honey. Serve over pancakes.

Prep Time: 20 minutes
Cook Time: 20 minutes

NUTRIENTS PER SERVING

1 pancake plus 2½ tablespoons topping = 1 serving

Calories:	135	Carbohydrate:	25g
Calories from Fat:	15%	Fiber:	2g
Total Fat:	2g	Protein:	5g
Saturated Fat:	<1g	Sodium:	150mg
Cholesterol:	<1mg		

Dietary Exchanges: 1 Starch, ½ Fruit, ½ Fat

Oatmeal Pumpkin Bread

- 1 cup quick-cooking oats
- 1 cup hot low-fat milk
- ¾ cup cooked or canned pumpkin
- 2 eggs, beaten
- ¼ cup margarine, melted
- 2 cups all-purpose flour
- 1 cup sugar
- 1 tablespoon baking powder
- 1 teaspoon ground cinnamon
- ¼ teaspoon ground nutmeg
- ¼ teaspoon salt
- 1 cup raisins
- ½ cup chopped pecans

Preheat oven to 350°F. In large bowl, combine oats and milk; allow to stand about 5 minutes. Stir in pumpkin, eggs and margarine. In separate bowl, mix together flour, sugar, baking powder, cinnamon, nutmeg and salt. Gradually add dry ingredients to oatmeal mixture; stir in raisins and nuts and mix well. Place in greased 9×5-inch loaf pan. Bake 55 to 60 minutes or until done. Cool on wire rack. *makes 1 loaf (16 slices)*

Favorite recipe from **The Sugar Association, Inc.**

NUTRIENTS PER SERVING

1 slice = 1 serving

Calories:	227	Carbohydrate:	39g
Calories from Fat:	26%	Fiber:	2g
Total Fat:	7g	Protein:	5g
Saturated Fat:	1g	Sodium:	179mg
Cholesterol:	28mg		

Dietary Exchanges: 2½ Starch, 1 Fat

Tip

Raisins will keep for several months if you wrap them securely in plastic wrap or store them in an airtight container at room temperature. They will keep even longer (up to one year) if you refrigerate them in a tightly covered container.

Eggs Primavera

4 small round loaves (4 inches each) whole wheat bread
Nonstick cooking spray
1½ cups chopped onions
¾ cup chopped yellow summer squash
¾ cup chopped zucchini
½ cup chopped red bell pepper
2 ounces snow peas, trimmed and cut diagonally into thirds
¼ cup finely chopped fresh parsley
1½ teaspoons finely chopped fresh thyme *or* ¾ teaspoon dried thyme leaves
1 teaspoon finely chopped fresh rosemary *or* ½ teaspoon dried rosemary
2 whole eggs
4 egg whites
¼ teaspoon black pepper
½ cup (2 ounces) shredded reduced-fat Swiss cheese

1. Preheat oven to 350°F. Slice top off each loaf of bread. Carefully hollow out each loaf, leaving sides and bottom ½ inch thick. Reserve centers for another use. Place loaves and tops, cut sides up, on baking sheet. Spray all surfaces with cooking spray; bake 15 minutes or until well toasted.

2. Spray large nonstick skillet with cooking spray and heat over medium heat until hot. Add onions; cook and stir 3 minutes or until soft. Add yellow squash, zucchini and bell pepper; cook and stir 3 minutes or until crisp-tender. Add snow peas and herbs; cook and stir 1 minute.

3. Whisk eggs, egg whites and black pepper in small bowl until blended. Add to vegetable mixture; gently stir until eggs begin to set. Sprinkle cheese over top; gently stir until cheese melts and eggs are set but not dry.

4. Fill each bread bowl with ¼ of egg mixture, about 1 cup. Place tops back on bread bowls before serving.

makes 4 servings

NUTRIENTS PER SERVING

¼ egg mixture with 1 loaf (1 ounce) of bread = 1 serving

Calories:	201	Carbohydrate:	23g
Calories from Fat:	26%	Fiber:	4g
Total Fat:	6g	Protein:	14g
Saturated Fat:	2g	Sodium:	336mg
Cholesterol:	114mg		

Dietary Exchanges: 1 Starch, 1 Vegetable, 1½ Lean Meat, ½ Fat

Apricot-Pecan Bran Muffins

- ⅓ cup pecan chips
- ⅓ cup plus 1 tablespoon sugar, divided
- 1 cup extra-fiber bran cereal
- 1 cup low-fat buttermilk
- 4 ounces baby food puréed prunes
- ½ cup chopped dried apricots or golden raisins
- 2 egg whites
- 2 teaspoons vanilla
- 1 cup all-purpose flour
- 2 teaspoons baking powder
- 1 teaspoon ground cinnamon
- ¼ teaspoon salt

1. Preheat oven to 400°F. Line 12 (2½-inch) muffin pan cups with paper baking cups. Set aside. Combine pecans and 1 tablespoon sugar in small bowl; set aside.

2. Combine cereal, buttermilk, prunes, apricots, egg whites and vanilla in medium bowl; stir to coat completely. Let stand 5 minutes.

3. Meanwhile, combine flour, ⅓ cup sugar, baking powder, cinnamon and salt in large mixing bowl. Make a well in center of flour mixture; add buttermilk mixture and stir just until blended.

4. Spoon batter into muffin cups. Sprinkle evenly with pecan mixture. Bake 20 minutes or until toothpick inserted into centers comes out clean. Cool in pan on wire rack 5 minutes. Remove from pan to rack. Serve warm or at room temperature. *makes 12 servings*

NUTRIENTS PER SERVING

1 (2½-inch) muffin = 1 serving

Calories:	129	Carbohydrate:	26g
Calories from Fat:	17%	Fiber:	4g
Total Fat:	3g	Protein:	4g
Saturated Fat:	<1g	Sodium:	193mg
Cholesterol:	<1mg		

Dietary Exchanges: 1 Starch, ½ Fruit, ½ Fat

Vegetable Soufflé in Pepper Cups

1 cup chopped broccoli
½ cup shredded carrot
¼ cup chopped onion
1 teaspoon dried basil leaves, crushed
½ teaspoon ground black pepper
2 teaspoons FLEISCHMANN'S® Original Margarine
2 tablespoons all-purpose flour
1 cup skim milk
1 cup EGG BEATERS® Healthy Real Egg Product
3 large red, green or yellow bell peppers, halved lengthwise

In nonstick skillet over medium-high heat, cook and stir broccoli, carrot, onion, basil and black pepper in margarine until vegetables are tender. Stir in flour until smooth. Gradually add milk, stirring constantly until thickened. Remove from heat; set aside.

In medium bowl, with electric mixer at high speed, beat Egg Beaters® until foamy, about 3 minutes. Gently fold into broccoli mixture; spoon into bell pepper halves. Place in 13×9-inch baking pan. Bake at 375°F for 30 to 35 minutes or until knife inserted in centers comes out clean. Garnish as desired and serve immediately.

makes 6 servings

NUTRIENTS PER SERVING

1 stuffed pepper half = 1 serving

Calories:	75	Carbohydrate:	10g
Calories from Fat:	16%	Fiber:	2g
Total Fat:	1g	Protein:	7g
Saturated Fat:	<1g	Sodium:	107mg
Cholesterol:	1mg		

Dietary Exchanges: 2 Vegetable, ½ Fat

Granola-Bran Muffins

1 cup boiling water
2½ cups whole bran cereal
1 egg, lightly beaten
1 egg white
2 cups buttermilk
¼ cup vegetable oil
½ cup finely chopped apple
2 cups all-purpose flour
1 cup sugar
½ cup quick-cooking rolled oats
½ cup wheat germ
2 teaspoons baking soda
½ teaspoon salt
1 cup raisins
½ cup chopped almonds, walnuts or pecans

Spray nonstick cooking spray in muffin cups or use paper liners. Preheat oven to 400°F. Pour boiling water over cereal in large bowl; cool. Stir in egg, egg white, buttermilk, oil and apple. Combine flour, sugar, oats, wheat germ, baking soda and salt in separate bowl. Stir in bran mixture. Stir in raisins and nuts. Fill prepared muffin cups ⅔ full. Bake 20 to 22 minutes or until wooden toothpick inserted in center comes out clean. *makes 36 muffins*

Favorite recipe from **Wisconsin Milk Marketing Board**

NUTRIENTS PER SERVING

1 muffin = 1 serving

Calories:	114	Carbohydrate:	20g
Calories from Fat:	22%	Fiber:	2g
Total Fat:	3g	Protein:	3g
Saturated Fat:	<1g	Sodium:	160mg
Cholesterol:	6mg		

Dietary Exchanges: 1 Starch, 1 Fat

Even though its name might suggest otherwise, buttermilk is a low-fat dairy product made from cow's milk. Originally, it was made from the liquid left after milk was churned into butter. Now, it is far more likely to be processed from nonfat or low-fat milk and treated with a special strain of bacteria to thicken it and add its characteristic tang.

Lean Meats

Southwestern Sloppy Joes

1 pound lean ground round
1 cup chopped onion
¼ cup chopped celery
¼ cup water
1 can (10 ounces) diced tomatoes and green chilies, undrained
1 can (8 ounces) no-salt-added tomato sauce
4 teaspoons brown sugar
½ teaspoon ground cumin
¼ teaspoon salt
9 whole wheat hamburger buns

1. Heat large nonstick skillet over high heat. Add beef, onion, celery and water. Reduce heat to medium. Cook and stir 5 minutes or until meat is no longer pink. Drain fat.

2. Stir in tomatoes and green chilies, tomato sauce, brown sugar, cumin and salt; bring to a boil over high heat. Reduce heat; simmer 20 minutes or until mixture thickens. Serve on whole wheat buns. Garnish as desired.

makes 9 servings

NUTRIENTS PER SERVING

1 bun plus ⅓ cup sloppy joe mix = 1 serving

Calories:	190	Carbohydrate:	26g
Calories from Fat:	19%	Fiber:	1g
Total Fat:	4g	Protein:	13g
Saturated Fat:	1g	Sodium:	413mg
Cholesterol:	15mg		

Dietary Exchanges: 1½ Starch, 1 Vegetable, 1 Lean Meat

Grilled Pork Tenderloin Medallions

PORK

2 tablespoons Pepper & Herb Rub (recipe follows)
12 pork tenderloin medallions (about 1 pound)
Olive oil-flavored nonstick cooking spray

1. Prepare Pepper & Herb Rub.

2. Prepare barbecue for direct grilling. Sprinkle rub evenly over both sides of pork, pressing lightly. Spray pork with nonstick cooking spray.

3. Place pork on grid over medium-hot coals. Grill, uncovered, 4 to 5 minutes per side or until pork is no longer pink in center. *makes 4 servings*

serving suggestion: Serve with steamed red potatoes and bell pepper strips.

Pepper & Herb Rub

1 tablespoon garlic salt
1 tablespoon dried basil leaves
1 tablespoon dried thyme leaves
1½ teaspoons cracked black pepper
1½ teaspoons dried rosemary
1 teaspoon paprika

Combine salt, basil, thyme, pepper, rosemary and paprika in small jar or resealable plastic food storage bag. Store in cool dry place up to 3 months.

NUTRIENTS PER SERVING

3 medallions = 1 serving

Calories:	145	Carbohydrate:	2g
Calories from Fat:	27%	Fiber:	1g
Total Fat:	4g	Protein:	24g
Saturated Fat:	1g	Sodium:	528mg
Cholesterol:	66mg		

Dietary Exchanges: 3 Lean Meat

Beef Stroganoff

1 large onion, cut lengthwise and thinly sliced
½ cup plain nonfat yogurt
½ cup reduced-fat sour cream
3 tablespoons snipped chives, divided
1 tablespoon all-purpose flour
2 teaspoons Dijon mustard
¼ teaspoon salt
⅛ teaspoon white pepper
1 teaspoon olive oil
1 pound boneless beef sirloin steak, cut in half lengthwise and sliced into ¼-inch pieces
6 ounces portobello or button mushrooms, sliced
8 ounces cooked mafalda or other wide noodles
12 ounces steamed baby carrots

1. Heat large nonstick skillet over low heat; add onion. Cover; cook, stirring occasionally, 10 minutes or until tender. Remove onion from skillet. Set aside.

2. Combine yogurt, sour cream, 2 tablespoons chives, flour, mustard, salt and pepper in small bowl. Set aside.

3. Heat oil in skillet over medium-high heat. Add beef and mushrooms; cook and stir 3 to 4 minutes or until beef is lightly browned. Return onion to skillet. Reduce heat to low. Stir in yogurt mixture until well blended and slightly thickened, about 2 minutes. Serve over noodles and with carrots. Sprinkle with remaining 1 tablespoon chives. Garnish as desired.

makes 6 servings

NUTRIENTS PER SERVING

Calories:	179	Carbohydrate:	14g
Calories from Fat:	24%	Fiber:	2g
Total Fat:	5g	Protein:	20g
Saturated Fat:	1g	Sodium:	190mg
Cholesterol:	45mg		

Dietary Exchanges: 2 Vegetable, 2½ Lean Meat

Tip

Today's beef is leaner than it used to be, with over 40% of beef cuts having no external fat at all. If you're trying to choose lean cuts of beef, look for "loin" or "round" in the name, such as sirloin, tenderloin or top round.

Glazed Pork Tenderloin (Calorie Watcher)

- 2 whole well-trimmed pork tenderloins (about 1½ pounds each)
- ½ cup currant jelly or canned jellied cranberry sauce
- 1 tablespoon prepared horseradish
- ½ cup chicken broth
- ¼ cup Rhine or other sweet white wine
- Salt (optional)
- Black pepper (optional)

1. Preheat oven to 325°F. Place tenderloins on meat rack in shallow roasting pan.

2. Combine jelly and horseradish in microwavable dish or small saucepan. Microwave at HIGH 1 minute or heat over low heat on rangetop until jelly is melted; mix well. Brush half of mixture over tenderloins.

3. Roast tenderloins 30 minutes. Turn tenderloins over; brush with remaining jelly mixture. Continue to roast 30 to 40 minutes, depending on thickness of tenderloins, or until meat thermometer registers 160°F. Transfer tenderloins to cutting board; tent with foil. Let stand 10 minutes.

4. Remove meat rack from roasting pan. To deglaze pan, pour chicken broth and wine into pan. Place over burners and cook over medium-high heat, stirring frequently and scraping up any browned bits, 4 to 5 minutes or until sauce is reduced to ½ cup.

5. Strain sauce; season to taste with salt and pepper, if desired.

6. Carve tenderloins into thin slices. Serve with sauce.

makes 6 servings

NUTRIENTS PER SERVING

Calories:	356	Carbohydrate:	18g
Calories from Fat:	23%	Fiber:	<1g
Total Fat:	9g	Protein:	47g
Saturated Fat:	3g	Sodium:	193mg
Cholesterol:	133mg		

Dietary Exchanges: 1 Fruit, 5½ Lean Meat

Lamb and Vegetable Kabobs on Saffron Rice

- 2 pounds lean boneless lamb, cut into 1½-inch cubes
- 1 *each* lime, lemon and orange peel
- ½ cup apple juice
- ¼ cup white wine vinegar
- 2 cloves garlic, sliced
- 1 small onion, chopped
- 1 teaspoon ground cumin
- 2 small zucchini, cut into 1-inch pieces
- 8 large pieces fresh pineapple
- 2 small onions, quartered
- 1 can (14½ ounces) reduced-sodium chicken broth
- 1½ cups uncooked rice
- ¹⁄₁₆ teaspoon ground saffron

1. Place lamb in resealable plastic food storage bag. Finely grate lime, lemon and orange peels. Combine grated peels, apple juice, vinegar, garlic, chopped onion and cumin in medium bowl. Pour half the marinade over lamb, turning to coat. Seal bag. Reserve other half of marinade. Marinate in refrigerator 4 hours or overnight, turning several times.

2. Place zucchini, pineapple and quartered onions in resealable plastic food storage bag. Pour reserved marinade over vegetable mixture, turning to coat. Seal bag. Marinate at room temperature 20 minutes, turning twice. Combine chicken broth and enough water to equal 3⅓ cups liquid in medium saucepan; add rice and saffron. Bring to a boil over high heat; reduce heat to low. Simmer, covered, 20 minutes or until rice is tender.

3. Remove lamb; discard marinade. Remove vegetables; reserve marinade. Thread lamb onto 8 skewers, alternating with zucchini, pineapple and quartered onions. Brush with reserved vegetable marinade. Arrange kabobs on rack of broiler pan sprayed with nonstick cooking spray. Broil, 4 inches from heat, 15 minutes or until desired doneness is reached, brushing with reserved marinade and turning every 5 minutes. Serve kabobs over rice. Garnish, if desired.

makes 8 servings

NUTRIENTS PER SERVING

1 kabob = 1 serving

Calories:	265	Carbohydrate:	34g
Calories from Fat:	16%	Fiber:	2g
Total Fat:	5g	Protein:	20g
Saturated Fat:	2g	Sodium:	77mg
Cholesterol:	48mg		

Dietary Exchanges: 2 Starch, 2 Lean Meat

Lamb and Vegetable Kabob on Saffron Rice

Beef Pot Roast

- 2½ pounds beef eye of round roast
- 1 can (14 ounces) fat-free reduced-sodium beef broth
- 2 cloves garlic
- 1 teaspoon herbs de Provence *or* ¼ teaspoon *each* rosemary, thyme, sage and savory
- 4 small turnips, peeled and cut into wedges
- 10 ounces fresh brussels sprouts, trimmed
- 8 ounces baby carrots
- 4 ounces pearl onions, skins removed
- 1 tablespoon water
- 2 teaspoons cornstarch

1. Heat large nonstick skillet over medium-high heat. Place roast, fat side down, in skillet. Cook until evenly browned. Remove roast from skillet; place in Dutch oven.

2. Pour broth into Dutch oven; bring to a boil over high heat. Add garlic and herbs de Provence. Cover and reduce heat; simmer 1½ hours.

3. Add turnips, brussels sprouts, carrots and onions to Dutch oven. Cover; cook 25 to 30 minutes or until vegetables are tender. Remove meat and vegetables and arrange on serving platter; cover with foil to keep warm.

4. Strain broth; return to Dutch oven. Stir water into cornstarch until smooth. Stir cornstarch mixture into broth. Bring to a boil over medium-high heat; cook and stir 1 minute or until thick and bubbly. Serve immediately with pot roast and vegetables. Garnish as desired.

makes 8 servings

NUTRIENTS PER SERVING

Calories:	261	Carbohydrate:	11g
Calories from Fat:	30%	Fiber:	2g
Total Fat:	9g	Protein:	35g
Saturated Fat:	3g	Sodium:	142mg
Cholesterol:	79mg		

Dietary Exchanges: 2 Vegetable, 4 Lean Meat

Sausage and Mushroom Pizza

New York-Style Pizza Crust (recipe follows)
1 large red bell pepper *or* ½ cup roasted red peppers, drained
3 cloves garlic, minced
1 teaspoon dried oregano leaves
2 teaspoons olive oil
4 to 6 ounces fat-free or reduced-fat sausage, cut into ⅛-inch-thick slices
5 medium mushrooms, thinly sliced
¼ cup chopped onion
½ cup (2 ounces) shredded part-skim mozzarella cheese or reduced-fat Monterey Jack cheese
Red pepper flakes

1. Prepare New York-Style Pizza Crust.

2. Preheat broiler. Cut bell pepper in half lengthwise. Discard stem and seeds. Place bell pepper halves, cut sides down, on baking sheet. Broil 1 to 2 inches from heat source 15 minutes or until skin turns black. Transfer bell pepper halves to plate and cover with plastic wrap. Let stand until cool enough to handle. Move oven rack to lowest position in oven and preheat oven to 500°F.

3. Peel skin from bell pepper halves and discard; coarsely chop bell pepper. Combine bell pepper, garlic and oregano in food processor; process until smooth. Set aside.

4. Brush prepared crust with oil. Bake 3 to 4 minutes or until surface is dry and crisp. Spread bell pepper mixture over crust, leaving 1-inch border. Top with sausage, mushrooms, onion and cheese. Bake about 6 minutes or until crust is golden brown. Sprinkle with red pepper flakes, and cut into 8 wedges. *makes 4 servings*

New York-Style Pizza Crust

⅔ cup warm water (110°F to 115°F)
1 teaspoon sugar
½ (¼-ounce) package rapid-rise or active dry yeast
1¾ cups all-purpose or bread flour
½ teaspoon salt
1 tablespoon cornmeal (optional)

1. Combine water and sugar in small bowl; stir to dissolve sugar. Sprinkle yeast on top; stir to combine. Let stand 5 to 10 minutes or until foamy.

2. Combine flour and salt in medium bowl. Stir in yeast mixture. Mix until mixture forms soft dough. Remove dough to lightly floured surface. Knead 5 minutes or until dough is smooth and elastic, adding additional flour, (1 tablespoon at a time) as needed. Place dough in medium bowl coated with nonstick cooking spray. Turn dough in bowl so top is coated with cooking spray; cover with towel or plastic wrap. Let rise in warm place 30 minutes or until doubled in bulk.

3. Punch dough down; place on lightly floured surface and knead about 2 minutes or until smooth. Pat dough into flat disc about 7 inches in diameter. Let rest 2 to 3 minutes. Pat and gently stretch dough from edges until dough seems to not stretch anymore. Let rest 2 to 3 minutes. Continue patting and stretching until dough is 12 to 14 inches in diameter.

4. Spray 12- to 14-inch pizza pan with nonstick spray; sprinkle with cornmeal, if desired. Press dough into pan.

makes 1 medium-thin 12-inch crust
or 1 very thin 14-inch crust

NUTRIENTS PER SERVING

2 wedges = 1 serving

Calories:	339	Carbohydrate:	52g
Calories from Fat:	20%	Fiber:	3g
Total Fat:	7g	Protein:	16g
Saturated Fat:	2g	Sodium:	573mg
Cholesterol:	26mg		

Dietary Exchanges: 3 Starch, 1 Vegetable, 1 Lean Meat, 1 Fat

Cajun Red Beans and Rice

1 can (15 ounces) red kidney beans, rinsed and drained
1 cup converted white rice
½ cup cubed 96% fat-free ham
1 can (about 14 ounces) defatted ⅓-less-salt chicken broth
1½ cups water
¼ cup tomato paste
1 bay leaf
1 teaspoon Cajun seasoning
⅛ teaspoon ground red pepper
½ teaspoon olive oil
1 medium green bell pepper, chopped
¾ cup chopped onion
¾ cup sliced celery
Hot pepper sauce (optional)

1. Combine beans, rice, ham, broth, water, tomato paste, bay leaf, Cajun seasoning and red pepper. Bring to a boil. Reduce heat to low; cover and simmer 15 minutes.

2. Meanwhile, heat oil in medium skillet over medium heat. Add bell pepper, onion and celery. Cook and stir 5 minutes; add to rice mixture. Continue to simmer 10 minutes or until rice is tender and flavors have blended. If mixture becomes dry, add small amount of water. Remove bay leaf; serve with hot pepper sauce, if desired. *makes 4 servings*

Prep and Cook Time: 28 minutes

NUTRIENTS PER SERVING

Calories:	335	Carbohydrate:	66g
Calories from Fat:	7%	Fiber:	9g
Total Fat:	3g	Protein:	17g
Saturated Fat:	<1g	Sodium:	611mg
Cholesterol:	5mg		

Dietary Exchanges: 4 Starch, 1 Vegetable, ½ Lean Meat

Italian-Style Meat Loaf

- 1 can (6 ounces) no-salt-added tomato paste
- ½ cup dry red wine plus ½ cup water *or* 1 cup water
- 1 teaspoon minced garlic
- ½ teaspoon dried basil leaves
- ½ teaspoon dried oregano leaves
- ¼ teaspoon salt
- 12 ounces lean ground round
- 12 ounces ground turkey breast
- 1 cup fresh whole wheat bread crumbs (2 slices whole wheat bread)
- ½ cup shredded zucchini
- ¼ cup cholesterol-free egg substitute *or* 2 egg whites

1. Preheat oven to 350°F. Combine tomato paste, wine, water, garlic, basil, oregano and salt in small saucepan. Bring to a boil; reduce heat to low. Simmer, uncovered, 15 minutes. Set aside.

2. Combine beef, turkey, bread crumbs, zucchini, egg substitute and ½ cup reserved tomato mixture in large bowl. Mix well. Shape into loaf; place into ungreased 9×5×3-inch loaf pan. Bake 45 minutes. Discard any drippings. Pour ½ cup remaining tomato mixture over top of loaf. Bake an additional 15 minutes. Place on serving platter. Cool 10 minutes before slicing. Garnish as desired.

makes 8 servings

NUTRIENTS PER SERVING

Calories:	144	Carbohydrate:	7g
Calories from Fat:	11%	Fiber:	1g
Total Fat:	2g	Protein:	19g
Saturated Fat:	1g	Sodium:	171mg
Cholesterol:	41mg		

Dietary Exchanges: 1 Vegetable, 2½ Lean Meat

Fresh ground turkey, sold in most supermarkets, can be used in place of ground beef to lower fat content in many recipes. Read the label carefully, though. If skin or fat is ground along with the meat, the amount of fat and cholesterol will increase.

Pork Tenderloin with Cabbage

- ¼ cup chicken broth or water
- 3 cups shredded red cabbage
- ¼ cup chopped onion
- 1 clove garlic, minced
- 1½ pounds pork tenderloin
- ¾ cup apple juice concentrate
- 3 tablespoons honey mustard
- 1½ tablespoons Worcestershire sauce

1. Preheat oven to 450°F. Pour chicken broth into shallow nonstick roasting pan; heat on rangetop over medium heat. Add cabbage, onion and garlic. Cook and stir 2 to 3 minutes or until cabbage wilts.

2. Add pork tenderloin. (If using two small tenderloins, place side-by-side.) Transfer roasting pan to oven. Roast for 10 minutes.

3. Meanwhile combine apple juice concentrate, mustard and Worcestershire in small bowl. Pour half the apple juice mixture over pork. Roast 10 minutes.

4. Remove pork from oven. Baste with half of remaining apple juice mixture; stir remaining mixture into cabbage. Return to oven and roast until meat thermometer inserted into center of pork registers 160°F, about 15 to 20 minutes.

5. Remove pork from oven and let stand 5 minutes. Slice and serve with cabbage and pan juices.

makes 6 servings

NUTRIENTS PER SERVING

Calories:	227	Carbohydrate:	21g
Calories from Fat:	18%	Fiber:	1g
Total Fat:	4g	Protein:	24g
Saturated Fat:	1g	Sodium:	145mg
Cholesterol:	66mg		

Dietary Exchanges: ½ Fruit, 1 Vegetable, 3 Lean Meat

Lasagna

- 1 teaspoon olive oil
- 2 cloves garlic, minced
- 2 cans (14 ounces each) no-salt-added Italian-style tomatoes, undrained
- ½ teaspoon dried Italian seasoning
- 8 ounces lean ground beef
- 1 large onion, chopped
- 8 ounces fresh mushrooms, sliced
- 2 zucchini, shredded
- 8 ounces uncooked lasagna noodles
- 1 cup 1% low-fat cottage cheese
- 1 cup nonfat ricotta cheese
- 1 cup (4 ounces) shredded part-skim mozzarella cheese, divided
- 2 egg whites
- 2 tablespoons Parmesan cheese

1. Heat oil in large nonstick skillet over medium heat. Add garlic; cook 1 minute. Add tomatoes and seasoning; bring to a boil. Reduce heat; simmer, uncovered, 20 to 25 minutes or until sauce thickens.

2. Heat large nonstick skillet over medium heat. Add beef and onion; cook and stir until beef is browned and onion is tender. Drain. Stir in mushrooms and zucchini; cook and stir 5 to 10 minutes or until tender.

3. Cook noodles according to package directions, omitting salt. Drain. Rinse under cold water; drain well. Combine cottage cheese, ricotta cheese, ½ cup mozzarella cheese and egg whites in medium bowl.

4. Preheat oven to 350°F. Spray 13×9-inch baking pan with nonstick cooking spray. Place layer of noodles in bottom of pan. Spread half of beef mixture over noodles. Top with half of cheese mixture and noodles. Repeat layering process, ending with noodles. Pour tomato mixture over noodles. Sprinkle with remaining ½ cup mozzarella and Parmesan cheese. Cover; bake 30 minutes. Uncover; bake 10 to 15 minutes or until heated through. Let stand 10 minutes before serving. Garnish as desired.

makes 8 servings

NUTRIENTS PER SERVING

Calories:	223	Carbohydrate:	23g
Calories from Fat:	22%	Fiber:	3g
Total Fat:	6g	Protein:	21g
Saturated Fat:	2g	Sodium:	302mg
Cholesterol:	22mg		

Dietary Exchanges: 1 Starch, 1 Vegetable, 2 Lean Meat

Mustard-Crusted Roast Pork

3 tablespoons Dijon mustard
4 teaspoons minced garlic, divided
2 whole well-trimmed pork tenderloins (about 1 pound each)
2 tablespoons dried thyme leaves
1 teaspoon black pepper
½ teaspoon salt
1 pound asparagus spears, ends trimmed
2 red or yellow bell peppers (or one of each), cut lengthwise into ½-inch-wide strips
1 cup fat-free reduced-sodium chicken broth, divided

1. Preheat oven to 375°F. Combine mustard and 3 teaspoons garlic in small bowl. Place tenderloins on waxed paper; spread mustard mixture evenly over top and sides of both tenderloins. Combine thyme, black pepper and salt in small bowl; reserve 1 teaspoon mixture. Sprinkle remaining mixture evenly over tenderloins, patting so that seasoning adheres to mustard. Place tenderloins on rack in shallow roasting pan. Roast 25 minutes.

2. Arrange asparagus and bell peppers in single layer in shallow casserole or 13×9-inch baking pan. Add ¼ cup broth, reserved thyme mixture and remaining 1 teaspoon garlic; toss to coat.

3. Roast vegetables in oven, alongside pork tenderloins, 15 to 20 minutes or until thermometer inserted into center of pork registers 160°F and vegetables are tender. Transfer tenderloins to carving board; tent with foil and let stand 5 minutes. Arrange vegetables on serving platter, reserving juices in dish; cover and keep warm. Add remaining ¾ cup broth and juices in dish to roasting pan. Place over range-top burner(s); simmer 3 to 4 minutes over medium-high heat or until juices are reduced to ¾ cup, stirring frequently. Carve tenderloin crosswise into ¼-inch slices; arrange on serving platter. Spoon juices over tenderloin and vegetables. *makes 8 servings*

NUTRIENTS PER SERVING

Calories:	182	Carbohydrate:	8g
Calories from Fat:	23%	Fiber:	1g
Total Fat:	5g	Protein:	27g
Saturated Fat:	2g	Sodium:	304mg
Cholesterol:	65mg		

Dietary Exchanges: 1 Vegetable, 3 Lean Meat

Beef Barley Soup

Nonstick cooking spray
¾ pound boneless beef top round, excess fat trimmed, cut into ½-inch pieces
3 cans (about 14 ounces each) defatted low-sodium beef broth*
1 can (14½ ounces) no-salt-added tomatoes
2 cups ½-inch unpeeled potato cubes
1½ cups ½-inch green bean slices
1 cup chopped onion
1 cup sliced carrots
½ cup pearled barley
1 tablespoon cider vinegar
2 teaspoons caraway seeds, lightly crushed
2 teaspoons dried marjoram leaves, crushed
2 teaspoons dried thyme leaves, crushed
½ teaspoon salt
½ teaspoon black pepper

**To defat beef broth, skim fat from surface of broth with spoon. Or, place can of broth in refrigerator at least 2 hours ahead of time. Before using, remove fat that has hardened on surface of broth.*

Coat large saucepan with cooking spray; heat over medium heat. Add beef; cook and stir until browned on all sides. Add remaining ingredients; bring to a boil over high heat. Reduce heat to low. Simmer, covered, about 2 hours or until beef is fork-tender, uncovering saucepan during last 30 minutes of cooking. *makes 4 servings*

NUTRIENTS PER SERVING

Calories:	447	Carbohydrate:	59g
Calories from Fat:	11%	Fiber:	9g
Total Fat:	6g	Protein:	42g
Saturated Fat:	1g	Sodium:	432mg
Cholesterol:	76mg		

Dietary Exchanges: 3 Starch, 2 Vegetable, 3½ Lean Meat

Tip

Barley is rich in both soluble and insoluble fiber. A recent study suggests that barley may also have a cholesterol-lowering effect similar to oat bran.

Pulled Pork Barbecue

- 1 whole pork tenderloin, (about 1 pound), all fat trimmed
- 1 teaspoon chili powder
- ½ teaspoon garlic powder
- Vegetable cooking spray
- ½ cup finely chopped onion
- 1½ teaspoons minced garlic
- 1 can (15 ounces) crushed tomatoes, undrained
- 1 tablespoon cider vinegar
- 1 tablespoon prepared mustard
- 1 to 2 teaspoons chili powder
- ¼ teaspoon maple extract
- ¼ teaspoon liquid smoke
- 2½ teaspoons EQUAL® FOR RECIPES *or* 8 packets EQUAL® sweetener *or* ⅓ cup EQUAL® SPOONFUL™
- Salt and pepper
- 6 multigrain hamburger buns, toasted

• Rub pork with 1 teaspoon chili powder and garlic powder; place in baking pan. Bake in preheated 425°F oven until pork is well browned and juices run clear, 30 to 40 minutes. Let stand 10 to 15 minutes. Cut into 2- to 3-inch slices; shred slices into bite-size pieces with fork.

• Spray medium saucepan with cooking spray; heat over medium heat until hot. Sauté onion and garlic until tender, about 5 minutes. Add tomatoes, vinegar, mustard, chili powder, maple extract and liquid smoke to saucepan; heat to boiling. Reduce heat and simmer, uncovered, until medium sauce consistency, 10 to 15 minutes. Stir in Equal®. Season to taste with salt and pepper. Stir pork into sauce; cook until hot, 2 to 3 minutes. Spoon mixture into buns.

makes 6 servings

NUTRIENTS PER SERVING

Calories:	289	Carbohydrate:	33g
Calories from Fat:	22%	Fiber:	4g
Total Fat:	7g	Protein:	23g
Saturated Fat:	2g	Sodium:	457mg
Cholesterol:	57mg		

Dietary Exchanges: 2 Starch, ½ Vegetable, 2 Lean Meat

Vegetable Beef Noodle Soup

8 ounces beef stew meat, cut into ½-inch pieces
¾ cup unpeeled cubed potato (1 medium)
½ cup sliced carrot
1 tablespoon balsamic vinegar
¾ teaspoon dried thyme leaves
¼ teaspoon black pepper
2½ cups fat-free reduced-sodium beef broth
1 cup water
¼ cup prepared chili sauce or ketchup
2 ounces uncooked thin egg noodles
¾ cup jarred or canned pearl onions, rinsed and drained
¼ cup frozen peas

1. Heat large saucepan over high heat until hot; add beef. Cook 3 minutes or until browned on all sides, stirring occasionally. Remove from pan.

2. Cook potato, carrot, vinegar, thyme and pepper 3 minutes in same saucepan over medium heat. Add beef broth, water and chili sauce. Bring to a boil over medium-high heat; add beef. Reduce heat to medium-low; simmer, covered, 30 minutes or until meat is almost fork-tender.

3. Bring beef mixture to a boil over medium-high heat. Add pasta; cook, covered, 7 to 10 minutes or until pasta is tender, stirring occasionally. Add onions and peas; heat 1 minute. Serve immediately. *makes 6 servings*

NUTRIENTS PER SERVING

1½ cups = 1 serving

Calories:	182	Carbohydrate:	24g
Calories from Fat:	14%	Fiber:	1g
Total Fat:	3g	Protein:	15g
Saturated Fat:	1g	Sodium:	258mg
Cholesterol:	28mg		

Dietary Exchanges: 1 Starch, 1 Vegetable, 1½ Lean Meat

Thai-Style Pork Kabobs

⅓ cup reduced-sodium soy sauce
2 tablespoons fresh lime juice
2 tablespoons water
2 teaspoons hot chili oil*
2 cloves garlic, minced
1 teaspoon minced fresh ginger
12 ounces well-trimmed pork tenderloin
1 red or yellow bell pepper, cut into ½-inch chunks
1 red or sweet onion, cut into ½-inch chunks
2 cups hot cooked rice

**If hot chili oil is not available, combine 2 teaspoons vegetable oil and ½ teaspoon red pepper flakes in small microwavable cup. Microwave at HIGH 1 minute. Let stand 5 minutes to infuse flavor.*

1. Combine soy sauce, lime juice, water, chili oil, garlic and ginger in medium bowl; reserve ⅓ cup mixture for dipping sauce. Set aside.

2. Cut pork tenderloin lengthwise in half; cut crosswise into 4-inch slices. Cut slices into ½-inch strips. Add to bowl with soy sauce mixture; toss to coat. Cover; refrigerate at least 30 minutes or up to 2 hours, turning once.

3. To prevent sticking, spray grid with nonstick cooking spray. Prepare coals for grilling.

4. Remove pork from marinade; discard marinade. Alternately weave pork strips and thread bell pepper and onion chunks onto eight 8- to 10-inch metal skewers.

5. Grill, covered, over medium-hot coals 6 to 8 minutes or until pork is no longer pink in center, turning halfway through grilling time. Serve with rice and reserved dipping sauce.

makes 4 servings

NUTRIENTS PER SERVING

Calories:	248	Carbohydrate:	30g
Calories from Fat:	16%	Fiber:	2g
Total Fat:	4g	Protein:	22g
Saturated Fat:	1g	Sodium:	271mg
Cholesterol:	49mg		

Dietary Exchanges: 1½ Starch, 1 Vegetable

Vegetable Spaghetti Sauce with Meatballs

- Nonstick cooking spray
- 1½ cups sliced fresh mushrooms
- ½ cup chopped onion plus 2 tablespoons finely chopped onion
- ½ cup chopped carrot
- ½ cup chopped green bell pepper
- 2 cloves garlic, minced
- 2 cans (14½ ounces each) no-salt-added stewed tomatoes, undrained
- 1 can (6 ounces) no-salt-added tomato paste
- 2½ teaspoons dried Italian seasoning, divided
- ½ teaspoon salt
- ¼ teaspoon black pepper
- 1 egg white
- 2 tablespoons fine dry bread crumbs
- 8 ounces 95% lean ground beef
- 4 cups hot cooked spaghetti

Preheat oven to 375°F. Coat large saucepan with cooking spray; heat over medium heat. Add mushrooms, ½ cup chopped onion, carrot, bell pepper and garlic. Cook and stir 4 to 5 minutes or until vegetables are crisp-tender. Stir in stewed tomatoes with liquid, tomato paste, 2 teaspoons Italian seasoning, salt and black pepper. Bring to a boil over medium-high heat. Reduce heat to medium-low. Cover and simmer 20 minutes, stirring occasionally.

Combine egg white, bread crumbs, remaining 2 tablespoons finely chopped onion and remaining ½ teaspoon Italian seasoning in medium bowl. Add beef; mix until well blended. Shape to form 16 meatballs. Place in 11×7-inch baking pan. Bake 18 to 20 minutes or until beef is no longer pink. Drain on paper towels.

Stir meatballs into sauce. Return sauce to a boil; reduce heat. Simmer, uncovered, about 10 minutes more or until sauce slightly thickens, stirring occasionally. Serve over spaghetti.

makes 4 servings

NUTRIENTS PER SERVING

Calories:	341	Carbohydrate:	56g
Calories from Fat:	13%	Fiber:	7g
Total Fat:	5g	Protein:	21g
Saturated Fat:	2g	Sodium:	381mg
Cholesterol:	25mg		

Dietary Exchanges: 3½ Starch, 3 Vegetable, 1½ Lean Meat

Zesty Skillet Pork Chops

1 teaspoon chili powder
½ teaspoon salt, divided
1¼ pounds lean pork chops, well trimmed of fat
2 cups diced tomatoes
1 cup chopped green, red or yellow bell pepper
¾ cup thinly sliced celery
½ cup chopped onion
1 tablespoon hot pepper sauce
1 teaspoon dried thyme leaves
Nonstick cooking spray
2 tablespoons finely chopped parsley

1. Rub chili powder and ¼ teaspoon salt evenly over one side of pork chops.

2. Combine tomatoes, bell pepper, celery, onion, pepper sauce and thyme in medium mixing bowl; stir to blend.

3. Lightly coat 12-inch nonstick skillet with cooking spray. Heat over medium-high heat until hot. Add pork chops, seasoned side down; cook 1 minute. Turn pork; top with tomato mixture.

4. Bring to a boil. Reduce heat and simmer, covered, 25 minutes or until pork is tender and mixture has thickened.

5. Transfer pork to serving plates. Increase heat; bring tomato mixture to a boil and cook 2 minutes or until most of the liquid has evaporated. Remove from heat. Stir in parsley and remaining ¼ teaspoon salt; spoon over pork.

makes 4 servings

NUTRIENTS PER SERVING

Calories: 172
Calories from Fat: . .34%
Total Fat: 7g
Saturated Fat: 2g
Cholesterol: 49mg
Carbohydrate: 9g
Fiber: 3g
Protein: 20g
Sodium: 387mg

Dietary Exchanges: 2 Vegetable, 2 Lean Meat

Purely Poultry

Washington Apple Turkey Gyros

- 1 cup vertically sliced onion
- 1 cup thinly sliced red bell pepper
- 1 cup thinly sliced green bell pepper
- 2 tablespoons lemon juice
- 1 tablespoon vegetable oil
- ½ pound cooked turkey breast, cut into thin strips
- 1 medium Washington Golden Delicious or Winesap apple, cored and thinly sliced
- 8 pita rounds, lightly toasted
- ½ cup plain low fat yogurt

Cook and stir onion, bell peppers and lemon juice in oil in nonstick skillet until crisp-tender; stir in turkey and cook until heated through. Remove from heat; stir in apple. Fold pita in half and fill with apple mixture; drizzle with yogurt. Repeat with remaining ingredients. Serve warm.

makes 6 servings

Favorite recipe from **Washington Apple Commission**

NUTRIENTS PER SERVING

Calories:	268	Carbohydrate:	40g
Calories from Fat:	13%	Fiber:	3g
Total Fat:	4g	Protein:	19g
Saturated Fat:	1g	Sodium:	322mg
Cholesterol:	33mg		

Dietary Exchanges: 1 Vegetable, 2 Lean Meat

Spaghetti Pie

4 ounces uncooked thin spaghetti
1 egg
¼ cup grated Parmesan cheese
1 teaspoon dried Italian seasoning
Nonstick cooking spray
⅔ cup reduced-fat ricotta cheese
½ pound 93% lean ground turkey
1 teaspoon chili powder
¼ teaspoon crushed fennel seeds
¼ teaspoon black pepper
⅛ teaspoon ground coriander
1 can (14½ ounces) diced tomatoes, undrained
1½ cups sliced fresh mushrooms
1 cup chopped onion
1 can (8 ounces) tomato sauce
¼ cup tomato paste
1 clove garlic, minced
2 teaspoons dried basil leaves
1 cup (4 ounces) shredded part-skim mozzarella cheese

1. Cook spaghetti according to package directions, omitting salt. Drain and rinse well under cold water; drain well.

2. Beat egg, Parmesan cheese and Italian seasoning lightly in medium bowl. Add spaghetti; blend well. Spray deep 9-inch pie plate with cooking spray. Press spaghetti mixture onto bottom and up side of pie plate. Spread ricotta cheese on spaghetti layer.

3. Preheat oven to 350°F. Combine turkey, chili powder, fennel seeds, pepper and coriander in medium bowl. Spray large nonstick skillet with cooking spray; heat over medium heat until hot. Brown turkey mixture until no longer pink, stirring to break up meat. Add remaining ingredients except mozzarella cheese. Cook and stir until mixture boils. Spoon mixture over ricotta cheese in pie plate.

4. Cover pie plate with foil. Bake 20 minutes. Remove foil. Sprinkle with mozzarella cheese; bake 5 minutes or until cheese is melted. Let stand before cutting and serving.

makes 6 servings

NUTRIENTS PER SERVING

Calories:	294	Carbohydrate:	31g
Calories from Fat:	24%	Fiber:	2g
Total Fat:	8g	Protein:	23g
Saturated Fat:	3g	Sodium:	797mg
Cholesterol:	67mg		

Dietary Exchanges: 1½ Starch, 2 Vegetable, 2 Lean Meat, ½ Fat

Lemon-Dijon Chicken with Potatoes

- 2 lemons, cut into halves
- ½ cup chopped fresh parsley
- 2 tablespoons Dijon mustard
- 4 cloves garlic, minced
- 2 teaspoons extra-virgin olive oil
- 1 teaspoon dried rosemary
- ¾ teaspoon black pepper
- ½ teaspoon salt
- 1 whole chicken (about 3½ pounds)
- 1½ pounds small red potatoes, cut into halves

Preheat oven to 350°F. Squeeze 3 tablespoons juice from lemons; reserve squeezed lemon halves. Combine parsley, lemon juice, mustard, garlic, oil, rosemary, pepper and salt in small bowl; blend well. Reserve 2 tablespoons mixture.

Place chicken on rack in baking pan; gently slide fingers between skin and meat of chicken breasts and drumsticks to separate skin from the meat, being careful not to tear skin. Spoon remaining parsley mixture between skin and meat (secure breast skin with wooden picks, if necessary) and place lemon halves in cavity of chicken. Bake 30 minutes.

Meanwhile, toss potatoes with reserved parsley mixture until coated. Arrange potatoes around chicken; bake 1 hour or until juices in chicken run clear and thermometer inserted into thickest part of thigh registers 180°F. Let chicken stand 10 minutes before removing skin and slicing. Sprinkle any accumulated parsley mixture over chicken and potatoes. *makes 6 servings*

NUTRIENTS PER SERVING

Calories:	294	Carbohydrate:	26g
Calories from Fat:	27%	Fiber:	3g
Total Fat:	9g	Protein:	30g
Saturated Fat:	2g	Sodium:	348mg
Cholesterol:	84mg		

Dietary Exchanges: 2 Starch, 3 Lean Meat

Turkey Vegetable Crescent Pie

- 2 cans (about 14 ounces) fat-free reduced-sodium chicken broth
- 1 medium onion, diced
- 1¼ pounds turkey tenderloins, cut into ¾-inch pieces
- 3 cups diced red potatoes
- 1 teaspoon chopped fresh rosemary *or* ½ teaspoon dried rosemary
- ¼ teaspoon salt
- ⅛ teaspoon black pepper
- 1 bag (16 ounces) frozen mixed vegetables
- 1 bag (10 ounces) frozen mixed vegetables
- ⅓ cup fat-free (skim) milk plus additional if necessary
- 3 tablespoons cornstarch
- 1 package (8 ounces) refrigerated reduced-fat crescent rolls

1. Bring broth to a boil in large saucepan. Add onion; reduce heat and simmer 3 minutes. Add turkey; return to a boil. Reduce heat; cover and simmer 7 to 9 minutes or until turkey is no longer pink. Remove turkey from saucepan with slotted spoon; place in 13×9-inch baking dish.

2. Return broth to a boil. Add potatoes, rosemary, salt and pepper; simmer 2 minutes. Return to a boil and stir in mixed vegetables. Simmer, covered, 7 to 8 minutes or until potatoes are tender. Remove vegetables with slotted spoon. Drain in colander set over bowl; reserve broth. Transfer vegetables to baking dish with turkey.

3. Preheat oven to 375°F. Blend ⅓ cup milk with cornstarch in small bowl until smooth. Add enough milk to reserved broth to equal 3 cups. Heat in large saucepan over medium-high heat; whisk in cornstarch mixture, stirring constantly until mixture comes to a boil. Boil 1 minute; remove from heat. Pour over turkey-vegetable mixture in baking dish.

4. Roll out crescent roll dough and separate at perforations; arrange dough pieces decoratively over top of turkey-vegetable mixture. Bake 13 to 15 minutes or until crust is golden brown.

makes 8 servings

NUTRIENTS PER SERVING

Calories:	285	Carbohydrate:	37g
Calories from Fat:	19%	Fiber:	5g
Total Fat:	6g	Protein:	20g
Saturated Fat:	<1g	Sodium:	458mg
Cholesterol:	28mg		

Dietary Exchanges: 2 Starch, 1 Vegetable, 2 Lean Meat

Barbecue Chicken Pizza

- New York-Style Pizza Crust (recipe follows)
- 6 ounces boneless skinless chicken breasts
- 2 teaspoons olive oil
- ¼ to ⅓ cup barbecue sauce
- ½ medium red onion, thinly sliced
- ½ green bell pepper, diced
- ½ cup (2 ounces) shredded reduced-fat Monterey Jack cheese
- ¼ cup fresh cilantro leaves

1. Prepare New York-Style Pizza Crust. Preheat oven to 500°F.

2. Slice chicken into ¼-inch-thick strips. Bring 4 cups water to a boil in large saucepan over high heat. Stir in chicken; cover and remove from heat. Let stand 3 to 4 minutes or until chicken is no longer pink in center. Drain; set aside.

3. Brush oil evenly over prepared crust. Spread barbecue sauce over crust, leaving 1-inch border. Arrange onion slices over sauce. Top with chicken, bell pepper and cheese. Bake on bottom rack of oven 10 minutes or until crust is dark golden brown. Sprinkle with cilantro and cut into 8 wedges. *makes 4 servings*

New York-Style Pizza Crust

- ⅔ cup warm water (110° to 115°F)
- 1 teaspoon sugar
- ½ (¼-ounce) package rapid-rise or active dry yeast
- 1¾ cups all-purpose or bread flour
- ½ teaspoon salt
- 1 tablespoon cornmeal (optional)

1. Combine water and sugar in small bowl; stir to dissolve sugar. Sprinkle yeast on top; stir to combine. Let stand 5 to 10 minutes or until foamy.

2. Combine flour and salt in medium bowl. Stir in yeast mixture. Mix until mixture forms soft dough. Remove dough to lightly floured surface. Knead 5 minutes or until dough is smooth and elastic, adding additional flour, 1 tablespoon at a time, as needed. Place dough in medium bowl coated with nonstick cooking spray. Turn dough in

continued on page 122

Barbecue Chicken Pizza, continued

bowl so top is coated with cooking spray; cover with towel or plastic wrap. Let rise in warm place 30 minutes or until doubled in bulk.

3. Punch dough down; place on lightly floured surface and knead about 2 minutes or until smooth. Pat dough into flat disc about 7 inches in diameter. Let rest 2 to 3 minutes. Pat and gently stretch dough from edges until dough seems to not stretch anymore. Let rest 2 to 3 minutes. Continue patting and stretching until dough is 12 to 14 inches in diameter.

4. Spray 12- to 14-inch pizza pan with cooking spray; sprinkle with cornmeal, if desired. Press dough into pan.

makes 1 medium-thin 12-inch crust or 1 very thin 14-inch crust

NUTRIENTS PER SERVING

2 wedges = 1 serving

Calories:	338	Carbohydrate:	47g
Calories from Fat:	18%	Fiber:	2g
Total Fat:	7g	Protein:	21g
Saturated Fat:	2g	Sodium:	530mg
Cholesterol:	36mg		

Dietary Exchanges: 3 Starch, 2 Lean Meat

90's-Style Slow Cooker Coq Au Vin

- 2 packages BUTTERBALL® Boneless Skinless Chicken Breast Fillets
- 1 pound fresh mushrooms, sliced thick
- 1 jar (15 ounces) pearl onions, drained
- ½ cup dry white wine
- 1 teaspoon thyme leaves
- 1 bay leaf
- 1 cup chicken broth
- ⅓ cup flour
- ½ cup chopped fresh parsley

SLOW COOKER DIRECTIONS

Place chicken, mushrooms, onions, wine, thyme and bay leaf into slow cooker. Combine chicken broth and flour; pour into slow cooker. Cover and cook 5 hours on low setting. Add parsley. Serve over wild rice pilaf, if desired.

makes 8 servings

Preparation Time: 30 minutes plus cooking time

NUTRIENTS PER SERVING

Calories:	192	Carbohydrate:	9g
Calories from Fat:	17%	Fiber:	1g
Total Fat:	3g	Protein:	27g
Saturated Fat:	1g	Sodium:	722mg
Cholesterol:	69mg		

Dietary Exchanges: 1 Vegetable, 3 Lean Meat

Less fat and less preparation time make this flavorful recipe even more appealing than the traditional version of this French dish.

Roast Turkey with Cranberry Stuffing

- 1 loaf (12 ounces) Italian or French bread, cut into ½-inch cubes
- 2 tablespoons margarine
- 1½ cups chopped onion
- 1½ cups chopped celery
- 2 teaspoons poultry seasoning
- 1 teaspoon dried thyme leaves
- ½ teaspoon dried rosemary, crushed
- ¼ teaspoon salt
- ¼ teaspoon black pepper
- 1 cup coarsely chopped fresh cranberries
- 1 tablespoon sugar
- ¾ cup fat-free reduced-sodium chicken broth
- 1 turkey (8 to 10 pounds)
- Fresh rosemary sprigs for garnish (optional)

1. Preheat oven to 375°F. Arrange bread on two 15×10-inch jelly-roll pans. Bake 12 minutes or until lightly toasted. *Reduce oven temperature to 350°F.*

2. Melt margarine in large saucepan over medium heat. Add onion and celery; cook and stir 8 minutes or until tender. Remove from heat. Add bread cubes, poultry seasoning, thyme, rosemary, salt and pepper; mix well. Combine cranberries and sugar in small bowl; add to bread mixture. Drizzle chicken broth evenly over mixture; toss.

3. Remove giblets from turkey. Rinse turkey and cavity in cold water; pat dry with paper towels. Fill turkey cavity loosely with stuffing. Place remaining stuffing in casserole sprayed with nonstick cooking spray. Cover; refrigerate.

4. Spray roasting pan with nonstick cooking spray. Place turkey, breast side up, on rack in roasting pan. Bake 3 hours or until thermometer inserted into thickest part of thigh registers 185°F and juices run clear. Transfer turkey to serving platter. Cover loosely with foil; let stand 20 minutes. Place covered casserole of stuffing in oven. *Increase temperature to 375°F.* Bake 25 to 30 minutes or until hot.

5. Remove turkey skin; discard. Slice turkey; serve with stuffing. Garnish as desired.

makes 20 servings

NUTRIENTS PER SERVING

Calories:	220	Carbohydrate:	12g
Calories from Fat:	26%	Fiber:	<1g
Total Fat:	6g	Protein:	28g
Saturated Fat:	2g	Sodium:	223mg
Cholesterol:	68mg		

Dietary Exchanges: 1 Starch, 3 Lean Meat

Mexican Tortilla Soup

- Nonstick cooking spray
- 2 pounds boneless skinless chicken breasts, cut into ½-inch strips
- 4 cups diced carrots
- 2 cups sliced celery
- 1 cup chopped onion
- 1 cup chopped green bell pepper
- 4 cloves garlic, minced
- 1 jalapeño pepper,* seeded and sliced
- 1 teaspoon dried oregano leaves
- ½ teaspoon ground cumin
- 8 cups fat-free reduced-sodium chicken broth
- 1 large tomato, seeded and chopped
- 4 to 5 tablespoons lime juice
- 2 (6-inch) corn tortillas, cut into ¼-inch strips
- Salt (optional)
- 3 tablespoons finely chopped fresh cilantro

**Jalapeño peppers can sting and irritate the skin; wear rubber gloves when handling peppers and do not touch eyes. Wash hands after handling.*

1. Preheat oven to 350°F. Spray large nonstick Dutch oven with cooking spray; heat over medium heat. Add chicken; cook and stir about 10 minutes or until browned and no longer pink. Add carrots, celery, onion, bell pepper, garlic, jalapeño pepper, oregano and cumin; cook and stir over medium heat 5 minutes.

2. Stir in chicken broth, tomato and lime juice; heat to a boil. Reduce heat to low; cover and simmer 15 to 20 minutes.

3. Meanwhile, spray tortilla strips lightly with cooking spray; sprinkle very lightly with salt, if desired. Place on baking sheet. Bake about 10 minutes or until browned and crisp, stirring occasionally.

4. Stir cilantro into soup. Ladle soup into bowls; top with tortilla strips.

makes 8 servings

NUTRIENTS PER SERVING

Calories:	184	Carbohydrate:	16g
Calories from Fat:	15%	Fiber:	4g
Total Fat:	3g	Protein:	23g
Saturated Fat:	1g	Sodium:	132mg
Cholesterol:	58mg		

Dietary Exchanges: 2 Vegetable, 2½ Lean Meat

Beefy Turkey and Noodles

- Nonstick cooking spray
- 8 ounces lean ground turkey
- 1 package (8 ounces) sliced fresh mushrooms
- 1 cup chopped onion
- 1 cup chopped green bell pepper
- 1½ cups water
- ½ can (6 ounces) no-salt-added tomato paste
- 1 tablespoon beef bouillon granules
- 1 teaspoon dried Italian seasoning
- 1 teaspoon Worcestershire sauce
- ¼ teaspoon granulated sugar
- 5 ounces uncooked yolk-free egg noodles

1. Spray large nonstick skillet with cooking spray. Heat over high heat until hot. Add turkey. Brown over medium-high heat 6 to 8 minutes or until no longer pink, stirring to separate turkey; drain fat. Remove turkey from skillet; set aside.

2. Add mushrooms to skillet; cook 3 minutes. Add onion and bell pepper; cook 5 minutes or until onion is tender. Add water, tomato paste, bouillon granules, Italian seasoning, Worcestershire, sugar and turkey; blend well. Bring to a boil. Reduce heat to low; simmer, covered, 20 minutes.

3. Meanwhile, cook noodles according to package directions, omitting salt. Drain. Add to skillet; stir to combine. Remove from heat. Let stand 5 minutes before serving. Garnish as desired.

makes 4 servings

NUTRIENTS PER SERVING

Calories:	272	Carbohydrate:	40g
Calories from Fat:	20%	Fiber:	3g
Total Fat:	6g	Protein:	17g
Saturated Fat:	1g	Sodium:	721mg
Cholesterol:	45mg		

Dietary Exchanges: 2 Starch, 2 Vegetable, 1½ Lean Meat

Mediterranean Chicken Kabobs

- 2 pounds boneless skinless chicken breasts or chicken tenders, cut into 1-inch pieces
- 1 small eggplant, peeled and cut into 1-inch pieces
- 1 medium zucchini, cut crosswise into ½-inch slices
- 2 medium onions, each cut into 8 wedges
- 16 medium mushrooms, stems removed
- 16 cherry tomatoes
- 1 cup fat-free reduced-sodium chicken broth
- ⅔ cup balsamic vinegar
- 3 tablespoons olive oil or vegetable oil
- 2 tablespoons dried mint leaves
- 4 teaspoons dried basil leaves
- 1 tablespoon dried oregano leaves
- 2 teaspoons grated lemon peel
- Chopped fresh parsley (optional)
- 4 cups hot cooked couscous

1. Alternately thread chicken, eggplant, zucchini, onions, mushrooms and tomatoes onto 16 metal skewers; place in large glass baking dish.

2. Combine chicken broth, vinegar, oil, mint, basil and oregano in small bowl; pour over kabobs. Cover; marinate in refrigerator 2 hours, turning kabobs occasionally.

3. Broil kabobs 6 inches from heat source 10 to 15 minutes or until chicken is no longer pink in center, turning kabobs halfway through cooking time. Or, grill kabobs on covered grill over medium-hot coals 10 to 15 minutes or until chicken is no longer pink in center, turning kabobs halfway through cooking time. Stir lemon peel and parsley, if desired, into couscous; serve with kabobs.

makes 8 servings

NUTRIENTS PER SERVING

2 kabobs plus ½ cup couscous = 1 serving

Calories:	300	Carbohydrate:	32g
Calories from Fat:	16%	Fiber:	4g
Total Fat:	5g	Protein:	31g
Saturated Fat:	1g	Sodium:	79mg
Cholesterol:	69mg		

Dietary Exchanges: 1 Starch, 3 Vegetable, 3 Lean Meat

Quick and Hearty Pizza

CRUST

- ½ cup warm water
- 1 package fast-rising active dry yeast
- 2 teaspoons vegetable oil
- ¼ teaspoon salt
- ½ cup whole wheat flour
- 1 cup all-purpose flour
- Olive oil-flavored nonstick cooking spray

TOPPING

- Nonstick cooking spray
- 1 cup sliced mushrooms
- 1 clove garlic, thinly sliced
- 2 tablespoons water
- 1 can (8 ounces) no-salt-added tomato sauce
- ½ teaspoon fresh basil, chopped
- ⅛ teaspoon black pepper
- 1 green bell pepper, seeded and sliced into rings
- ½ cup Italian-style smoked turkey sausage, sliced
- ½ cup (2 ounces) shredded part-skim mozzarella cheese

1. Preheat oven to 450°F. Pour ½ cup warm water and yeast into medium bowl. Stir until completely dissolved. Using wire whisk, stir in oil, salt and whole wheat flour until blended. Using wooden spoon, stir in all-purpose flour until soft dough forms. Turn dough out onto lightly floured surface. Knead dough 5 minutes.

2. Spray medium bowl with olive oil-flavored nonstick cooking spray. Place dough in bowl; cover with plastic wrap. Let dough rest 15 to 20 minutes. Spray 12-inch pizza pan with nonstick cooking spray. Roll out dough to about ½-inch thickness. Press dough into prepared pizza pan; set aside.

3. For topping, spray large skillet with cooking spray. Add mushrooms, garlic and 2 tablespoons water. Cook and stir over high heat 5 minutes or until water evaporates and mushrooms are lightly browned. Reduce heat to low. Add tomato sauce, basil and black pepper; mix well. Spread sauce on pizza crust. Top sauce with pepper rings, sausage and cheese. Bake 12 to 14 minutes or until cheese is golden.

makes 4 servings

NUTRIENTS PER SERVING

Calories:	348	Carbohydrate:	51g
Calories from Fat:	23%	Fiber:	6g
Total Fat:	9g	Protein:	16g
Saturated Fat:	2g	Sodium:	401mg
Cholesterol:	25mg		

Dietary Exchanges: 3 Starch, 1 Vegetable, 1 Lean Meat, 1 Fat

Jerk Chicken and Pasta

- Jerk Sauce (recipe follows)
- 12 ounces boneless skinless chicken breasts
- Nonstick cooking spray
- 1 cup canned fat-free reduced-sodium chicken broth
- 1 green bell pepper, sliced
- 2 green onions with tops, sliced
- 8 ounces uncooked fettuccine, cooked and kept warm
- Grated Parmesan cheese (optional)

1. Spread Jerk Sauce on both sides of chicken. Place in glass dish; refrigerate, covered, 15 to 30 minutes.

2. Spray medium skillet with cooking spray. Heat over medium heat until hot. Add chicken; cook 5 to 10 minutes or until browned and no longer pink in center. Add broth, bell pepper and onions; bring to a boil. Reduce heat; simmer, uncovered, 5 to 7 minutes or until vegetables are crisp-tender and broth is reduced to thin sauce. Remove chicken from skillet; cut into slices. Toss fettuccine, chicken and vegetable mixture in large bowl. Sprinkle with Parmesan, if desired. *makes 4 servings*

Jerk Sauce

- ¼ cup loosely packed fresh cilantro
- 2 tablespoons coarsely chopped fresh ginger
- 2 tablespoons black pepper
- 2 tablespoons lime juice
- 3 cloves garlic
- 1 tablespoon ground allspice
- ½ teaspoon curry powder
- ¼ teaspoon ground cloves
- ⅛ teaspoon ground red pepper

Combine all ingredients in food processor or blender; process until thick paste. *makes about ¼ cup*

NUTRIENTS PER SERVING

Calories:	345	Carbohydrate:	50g
Calories from Fat:	9%	Fiber:	1g
Total Fat:	4g	Protein:	27g
Saturated Fat:	1g	Sodium:	51mg
Cholesterol:	52mg		

Dietary Exchanges: 3 Starch, 2½ Lean Meat

Veggie & Chicken Nuggets

- 1 bag (16 ounces) BIRDS EYE® frozen Farm Fresh Mixtures Broccoli, Cauliflower & Carrots
- 1 box (5½ ounces) seasoning & coating mix for chicken (2 packets)
- ¼ to ½ teaspoon garlic powder
- 1 pound boneless, skinless chicken breast halves, cut into 1½- to 2-inch pieces

• Preheat oven to 400°F.

• Rinse vegetables under warm water to thaw; drain.

• In small bowl, mix coating mix with garlic powder; place ½ of mixture in resealable plastic food storage bag. Add vegetables; shake until evenly coated. Place in single layer on ungreased 15×10-inch baking pan.

• Moisten chicken with water. Add remaining coating mixture and chicken to same bag; shake until evenly coated.

• Place chicken on pan with vegetables, using additional baking pan if too crowded.

• Bake 10 to 15 minutes or until chicken is no longer pink in center. *makes 4 servings*

Prep Time: 5 minutes
Cook Time: 15 minutes

NUTRIENTS PER SERVING

Calories:	331	Carbohydrate:	35g
Calories from Fat:	19%	Fiber:	3g
Total Fat:	7g	Protein:	31g
Saturated Fat:	1g	Sodium:	1002mg
Cholesterol:	69mg		

Dietary Exchanges: 2 Starch, 1 Vegetable, 3 Lean Meat

Turkey Medallions with Marsala Mustard Sauce

¼ cup all-purpose flour
¼ teaspoon salt
¼ teaspoon pepper
1 pound turkey tenderloins, cut into ¾-inch medallions
½ cup marsala wine
¼ cup reduced sodium chicken bouillon
2 teaspoons Dijon-style mustard
1 tablespoon olive oil
1 clove garlic, minced

Combine flour, salt and pepper in 9-inch pie plate. Dredge turkey medallions in flour mixture. Reserve 2 teaspoons remaining flour mixture and combine with wine, bouillon and mustard.

Heat oil over medium heat in large nonstick skillet. Add medallions. Cook and stir 4 to 5 minutes per side or until turkey is no longer pink in center. Remove medallions from pan and keep warm.

Over medium heat cook and stir garlic until lightly browned. Add wine mixture, stirring constantly 1 minute or until mixture thickens.

To serve, pour sauce over medallions.

makes 4 servings

Favorite recipe from **National Turkey Federation**

NUTRIENTS PER SERVING

Calories:	190	Carbohydrate:	7g
Calories from Fat:	28%	Fiber:	<1g
Total Fat:	6g	Protein:	21g
Saturated Fat:	1g	Sodium:	224mg
Cholesterol:	45mg		

Dietary Exchanges: ½ Starch, 3 Lean Meat

Roast Turkey Breast with Spinach-Blue Cheese Stuffing

3½- to 4-pound boneless turkey breast, thawed
1 package (10 ounces) frozen chopped spinach, thawed and squeezed dry
2 ounces blue cheese or feta cheese
2 ounces reduced-fat cream cheese
½ cup finely chopped green onions
4½ teaspoons Dijon mustard
4½ teaspoons dried basil leaves
2 teaspoons dried oregano leaves
Black pepper to taste
Paprika

Preheat oven to 350°F. Coat roasting pan and rack with nonstick cooking spray.

Unroll turkey breast; rinse and pat dry. Place on sheet of plastic wrap and top with second sheet of plastic wrap. Pound turkey breast with flat side of meat mallet to create even piece about 1 inch thick. Remove skin from one side of turkey breast and turn meat over so skin side faces down.

Combine spinach, blue cheese, cream cheese, green onions, mustard, basil and oregano in medium bowl; mix well. Spread evenly over turkey breast. Fold or roll up turkey so skin is on top.

Carefully place turkey breast on rack; sprinkle with pepper and paprika. Bake 1½ hours or until no longer pink in center of breast. Remove from oven and let stand 10 minutes before removing skin and slicing. Cut into ¼-inch slices. *makes 14 servings*

NUTRIENTS PER SERVING

3 ounces = 1 serving

Calories:	135	Carbohydrate:	2g
Calories from Fat:	28%	Fiber:	1g
Total Fat:	4g	Protein:	22g
Saturated Fat:	2g	Sodium:	144mg
Cholesterol:	50mg		

Dietary Exchanges: 3 Lean Meat

Grilled Chicken, Rice & Veggies

3 ounces boneless skinless chicken breast
3 tablespoons reduced-fat Italian salad dressing, divided
½ cup fat-free reduced-sodium chicken broth
¼ cup uncooked rice
½ cup frozen broccoli and carrot blend, thawed

1. Place chicken and 1 tablespoon salad dressing in resealable plastic food storage bag. Seal bag; turn to coat. Marinate in refrigerator 1 hour.

2. Remove chicken from marinade; discard marinade. Grill chicken over medium-hot coals 8 to 10 minutes or until chicken is no longer pink in center.

3. Meanwhile, bring broth to a boil in small saucepan; add rice. Cover; reduce heat and simmer 15 minutes, stirring in vegetables during last 5 minutes of cooking. Remove from heat and stir in remaining 2 tablespoons dressing. Serve with chicken.

makes 1 serving

NUTRIENTS PER SERVING

Calories:	268	Carbohydrate:	25g
Calories from Fat:	23%	Fiber:	4g
Total Fat:	7g	Protein:	26g
Saturated Fat:	1g	Sodium:	516mg
Cholesterol:	54mg		

Dietary Exchanges: 1½ Starch, 1 Vegetable, 2 Lean Meat

recipe tip

Thaw chicken pieces in the refrigerator, allowing three to four hours per pound. Or, thaw them even quicker by immersing them in cold water. Leave them in their original packaging, and change the water frequently so the chicken stays cold. If you decide to use your microwave for defrosting, follow the manufacturer's directions. Make sure the edges of the chicken pieces don't begin to cook before the rest is completely thawed. And, any chicken thawed in cold water or in the microwave should be used immediately.

California Turkey Chili

- 1¼ cups chopped onion
- 1 cup chopped green bell pepper
- 2 cloves garlic, minced
- 3 tablespoons vegetable oil
- 1 can (28 ounces) kidney beans, drained
- 1 can (28 ounces) stewed tomatoes, undrained
- 1 cup red wine or water
- 3 cups cubed cooked California-grown turkey
- 1 tablespoon chili powder
- 1 tablespoon chopped cilantro *or* 1 teaspoon dried coriander
- 1 teaspoon crushed red pepper
- ½ teaspoon salt
- Shredded Cheddar cheese (optional)
- Additional chopped onion (optional)
- Chopped cilantro (optional)

Cook and stir onion, green pepper, garlic and oil in large saucepan over high heat until tender. Add beans, tomatoes with liquid, wine, turkey, chili powder, cilantro, red pepper and salt. Cover; simmer 25 minutes or until heated through. Top with cheese, onion or cilantro, if desired.

makes 6 servings

Favorite recipe from **California Poultry Federation**

NUTRIENTS PER SERVING

Calories:	372	Carbohydrate:	36g
Calories from Fat:	24%	Fiber:	10g
Total Fat:	10g	Protein:	30g
Saturated Fat:	2g	Sodium:	1007mg
Cholesterol:	48mg		

Dietary Exchanges: 2 Starch, 1 Vegetable, 3 Lean Meat, 1 Fat

Tip

Cilantro is another name for the green, lacy leaves of the coriander plant. The best way to store a bunch of this pungent herb is with its stems down in a glass of water and a plastic bag over its leaves. Change the water every few days.

Chicken Noodle Roll-Ups

- 9 uncooked lasagna noodles (about 9 ounces)
- 8 ounces boneless skinless chicken breasts, cut into chunks
- Nonstick cooking spray
- 2 cups finely chopped broccoli
- 2 cups 1% low-fat cottage cheese
- 1 egg
- 2 teaspoons snipped fresh chives
- ¼ teaspoon ground nutmeg
- ¼ teaspoon black pepper
- 1 tablespoon reduced-fat margarine
- 2 tablespoons all-purpose flour
- 1 cup ⅓-less-sodium chicken broth
- ½ cup fat-free (skim) milk
- ½ teaspoon dry mustard
- 1 medium tomato, seeded and chopped

1. Cook lasagna noodles according to package directions, omitting salt. Drain and rinse well under cold water. Place in single layer on aluminum foil.

2. Preheat oven to 375°F. Place chicken in food processor or blender; process until finely chopped. Spray large nonstick skillet with cooking spray; place over medium heat. Add chicken; cook 4 minutes or until chicken is no longer pink. Stir in broccoli; cook until broccoli is crisp-tender, about 3 minutes. Cool.

3. Combine cottage cheese, egg, chives, nutmeg and black pepper. Stir in chicken mixture. Spread a generous ⅓ cup filling over each lasagna noodle. Roll up noodles, starting at short end. Place filled rolls, seam side down, in 10×8-inch baking dish; set aside.

4. Melt margarine in small saucepan. Stir in flour; cook 1 minute. Whisk in chicken broth, milk and mustard. Cook, stirring constantly, until thickened. Pour sauce over filled rolls; sprinkle with tomato. Cover dish with foil. Bake 30 to 35 minutes or until filling is set.

makes 9 servings

NUTRIENTS PER SERVING

1 roll-up = 1 serving

Calories:	179	Carbohydrate:	17g
Calories from Fat:	22%	Fiber:	2g
Total Fat:	4g	Protein:	18g
Saturated Fat:	1g	Sodium:	291mg
Cholesterol:	46mg		

Dietary Exchanges: 1 Starch, 2 Lean Meat

Chicken Noodle Roll-Up

Turkey Meatloaf

- 1 tablespoon vegetable oil
- ¾ cup chopped onion
- ½ cup chopped celery
- 1 clove garlic, minced
- ⅔ cup fat-free reduced-sodium chicken broth or water
- ½ cup bulgur
- ½ cup cholesterol-free egg substitute
- 1 tablespoon reduced-sodium soy sauce
- ¼ teaspoon ground cumin
- ¼ teaspoon paprika
- ¼ teaspoon black pepper
- 8 tablespoons chili sauce, divided
- 1 pound ground turkey breast

1. Heat oil in medium skillet. Add onion, celery and garlic. Cook and stir 3 minutes over low heat. Add broth and bulgur. Bring to a boil. Reduce heat to low. Cover and simmer 10 to 15 minutes or until bulgur is tender and all liquid is absorbed. Transfer to large bowl; cool to lukewarm.

2. Preheat oven to 375°F. Stir egg substitute, soy sauce, cumin, paprika and pepper into bulgur. Add 6 tablespoons chili sauce and ground turkey. Stir until well blended.

3. Pat mixture into 8½×4½-inch loaf pan. Top with remaining 2 tablespoons chili sauce.

4. Bake meatloaf about 45 minutes or until browned and juices run clear. Let stand 10 minutes. Cut into 10 slices.

makes 5 servings

NUTRIENTS PER SERVING

2 slices = 1 serving

Calories:	197	Carbohydrate:	18g
Calories from Fat:	22%	Fiber:	4g
Total Fat:	5g	Protein:	20g
Saturated Fat:	<1g	Sodium:	437mg
Cholesterol:	36mg		

Dietary Exchanges: 1 Starch, 1 Vegetable, 2 Lean Meat

Sweet & Sour Chicken and Rice

- 1 pound chicken tenders
- 1 can (8 ounces) pineapple chunks, drained and juice reserved
- 1 cup uncooked rice
- 2 carrots, thinly sliced
- 1 green bell pepper, cut into 1-inch pieces
- 1 large onion, chopped
- 3 cloves garlic, minced
- 1 can (14½ ounces) reduced-sodium chicken broth
- ⅓ cup soy sauce
- 3 tablespoons sugar
- 3 tablespoons apple cider vinegar
- 1 tablespoon sesame oil
- 1½ teaspoons ground ginger
- ¼ cup chopped peanuts (optional)
- Chopped fresh cilantro (optional)

Preheat oven to 350°F. Spray 13×9-inch baking dish with nonstick cooking spray.

Combine chicken, pineapple, rice, carrots, bell pepper, onion and garlic in prepared dish.

Place broth, reserved pineapple juice, soy sauce, sugar, vinegar, sesame oil and ginger in small saucepan; bring to a boil over high heat. Remove from heat and pour over chicken mixture.

Cover tightly with foil and bake 40 to 50 minutes or until chicken is no longer pink in center and rice is tender. Sprinkle with peanuts and cilantro, if desired.

makes 6 servings

NUTRIENTS PER SERVING

Calories:	289	Carbohydrate:	45g
Calories from Fat:	10%	Fiber:	2g
Total Fat:	3g	Protein:	20g
Saturated Fat:	<1g	Sodium:	1166mg
Cholesterol:	32mg		

Dietary Exchanges: 2 Starch, 1 Fruit, 2 Lean Meat

The Californian

- 3 tablespoons reduced-fat cream cheese, softened
- 1 tablespoon chutney
- 4 slices pumpernickel bread
- 4 lettuce leaves
- ¾ pound thinly sliced deli chicken breast
- 1⅓ cups alfalfa sprouts
- 1 medium mango, peeled and sliced
- 1 pear, cored and sliced
- 4 strawberries

Combine cream cheese and chutney in small bowl; spread about 1 tablespoon onto each bread slice. Place 1 lettuce leaf over cream cheese mixture. Divide chicken evenly into 4 servings; place over lettuce. Arrange alfalfa sprouts over chicken; arrange mango and pear slices over sprouts. Garnish each open-faced sandwich with a strawberry.

makes 4 servings

NUTRIENTS PER SERVING

1 open-faced sandwich = 1 serving

Calories:	318	Carbohydrate:	36g
Calories from Fat:	17%	Fiber:	6g
Total Fat:	6g	Protein:	30g
Saturated Fat:	2g	Sodium:	304mg
Cholesterol:	72mg		

Dietary Exchanges: 1 Starch, 1½ Fruit, 3 Lean Meat

Tip

This flavorful sandwich is a perfect idea for a healthy meal when you're in a hurry.

Sensible Seafood

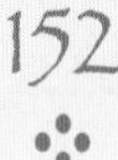

Seafood & Vegetable Stir-Fry

- 2 teaspoons olive oil
- ½ medium red or yellow bell pepper, cut into strips
- ½ medium onion, cut into small wedges
- 10 snow peas, trimmed and cut diagonally into halves
- 1 clove garlic, minced
- 6 ounces frozen cooked medium shrimp, thawed
- 2 tablespoons stir-fry sauce
- 1 cup hot cooked rice

1. Heat oil in large nonstick skillet over medium-high heat. Add vegetables; stir-fry 4 minutes. Add garlic; stir-fry 1 minute or until vegetables are crisp-tender.

2. Add shrimp and stir-fry sauce. Stir-fry 1 to 2 minutes or until hot. Serve over rice. *makes 2 servings*

NUTRIENTS PER SERVING

Calories:	279	Carbohydrate:	33g
Calories from Fat:	19%	Fiber:	2g
Total Fat:	6g	Protein:	22g
Saturated Fat:	1g	Sodium:	724mg
Cholesterol:	166mg		

Dietary Exchanges: 1½ Starch, 2 Vegetable, 2 Lean Meat

Today's Slim Tuna Stuffed Tomatoes

6 medium tomatoes
1 cup dry curd cottage cheese
½ cup plain low fat yogurt
¼ cup chopped cucumber
¼ cup chopped green bell pepper
¼ cup thinly sliced radishes
¼ cup chopped green onions
½ teaspoon dried basil leaves, crushed
⅛ teaspoon garlic powder
1 can (6½ ounces) tuna, packed in water, drained and flaked
Lettuce leaves

Cut each tomato into 6 wedges, cutting to, but not through, base of each tomato. Refrigerate. In medium bowl, combine cottage cheese and yogurt; mix well. Stir in remaining ingredients except lettuce leaves. Place tomatoes on individual lettuce-lined plates; spread wedges apart. Spoon cottage cheese mixture into center of each tomato. *makes 6 servings*

Favorite recipe from **Wisconsin Milk Marketing Board**

NUTRIENTS PER SERVING

Calories:	98	Carbohydrate:	9g
Calories from Fat:	12%	Fiber:	2g
Total Fat:	1g	Protein:	14g
Saturated Fat:	<1g	Sodium:	48mg
Cholesterol:	8mg		

Dietary Exchanges: 1 Vegetable, 1½ Lean Meat

Tip

Tomatoes should never be refrigerated before they are cut. Cold temperatures cause the flesh of the tomatoes to become mealy and lose its flavor. Store them at room temperature instead. And if you want to speed the ripening of unripened tomatoes, put them in a paper bag.

Hawaiian Shrimp Kabobs

1 can (6 ounces) pineapple juice
⅓ cup packed brown sugar
4 teaspoons cornstarch
1 tablespoon rice wine vinegar
1 tablespoon reduced-sodium soy sauce
1 clove garlic, minced
¼ teaspoon ground ginger
1 medium green bell pepper
1 medium red bell pepper
1 medium onion
1 cup fresh pineapple chunks
1 cup fresh mango* or papaya chunks (1 mango, peeled, cut into bite-size pieces)
1 pound raw large shrimp, peeled and deveined
2½ cups hot cooked white rice
Red onion rings and fresh herb sprigs (optional)

**1 peeled mango cut into bite-size pieces = 1 cup mango*

1. For sauce, combine juice, sugar, cornstarch, vinegar, soy sauce, garlic and ginger in saucepan. Cook over medium-high heat until mixture comes to a boil and thickens, stirring frequently; set aside.

2. Preheat broiler. Cut peppers and onion into 1-inch squares. Thread peppers, onion, pineapple, mango and shrimp onto 10 metal skewers. Place kabobs in large glass baking dish. Brush reserved sauce over kabobs.

3. Spray rack of broiler pan with nonstick cooking spray. Place kabobs on rack. Broil 3 to 4 inches from heat 3 minutes. Turn and brush with sauce; discard any remaining sauce. Broil 3 minutes more or until shrimp turn pink and opaque. Serve with rice. Garnish with onion rings and herbs, if desired. *makes 5 servings*

NUTRIENTS PER SERVING

2 kabobs plus ½ cup cooked rice = 1 serving

Calories:	318	Carbohydrate:	58g
Calories from Fat:	4%	Fiber:	3g
Total Fat:	1g	Protein:	18g
Saturated Fat:	<1g	Sodium:	275mg
Cholesterol:	139mg		

Dietary Exchanges: 2 Starch, 1 Fruit, 2 Vegetable, 1 Lean Meat

Caribbean Sea Bass with Mango Salsa

- 4 (4 ounces each) skinless sea bass fillets, about 1 inch thick
- 1 teaspoon Caribbean jerk seasoning
- Nonstick cooking spray
- 1 ripe mango, peeled, pitted and diced, *or* 1 cup diced drained bottled mango
- 2 tablespoons chopped fresh cilantro
- 2 teaspoons fresh lime juice
- 1 teaspoon minced fresh or bottled jalapeño pepper*

**Jalapeño peppers can sting and irritate the skin; wear rubber gloves when handling peppers and do not touch eyes. Wash hands after handling peppers.*

1. Prepare grill or preheat broiler. Sprinkle fish with seasoning; coat lightly with cooking spray. Grill fish over medium coals or broil 5 inches from heat for 4 to 5 minutes per side or until fish flakes easily with fork.

2. Meanwhile, combine mango, cilantro, lime juice and jalapeño pepper; mix well. Serve over fish.

makes 4 servings

Prep Time: 10 minutes
Cook Time: 10 minutes

NUTRIENTS PER SERVING

Calories:	146	Carbohydrate:	9g
Calories from Fat:	15%	Fiber:	1g
Total Fat:	2g	Protein:	21g
Saturated Fat:	1g	Sodium:	189mg
Cholesterol:	47mg		

Dietary Exchanges: ½ Fruit, 2 Lean Meat

Jerk seasoning is a dry blend of ingredients—traditionally chilies, thyme, garlic, onions, cinnamon, ginger, allspice and cloves. It was originally used in Jamaica to season such meats as pork and chicken. Today, we use this seasoning to add a particularly zippy flavor to all sorts of dishes.

Paella

- 1 pound littleneck clams
- 8 to 10 ounces sea scallops
- 6 ounces raw medium shrimp
- 4 teaspoons olive oil, divided
- 3¼ cups reduced-sodium chicken broth, divided
- 1 medium onion, finely chopped
- 3 cloves garlic, chopped
- 2 cups long-grain white rice
- 1 teaspoon dried thyme leaves, crushed
- ½ teaspoon saffron threads, crushed
- 1 pint cherry tomatoes, halved
- 1 cup frozen petit peas, thawed
- 1 tablespoon chopped fresh parsley

1. Discard any clams that remain open when tapped with fingers. To clean clams, scrub with stiff brush under cold running water. Soak clams in mixture of ⅓ cup salt to 1 gallon water 20 minutes. Drain water; repeat 2 more times. Slice sea scallops in half crosswise into rounds. Peel shrimp, leaving tails on if desired; devein.

2. Heat 1 teaspoon oil over medium-high heat in large saucepan. Add shrimp; cook, stirring occasionally, 3 minutes or until shrimp turn pink. Transfer to bowl; cover. Add scallops to saucepan; cook 2 minutes or until scallops are opaque. Transfer to bowl with shrimp. Add clams and ¼ cup broth to pan. Cover; boil 2 to 8 minutes or until clams open. Transfer clams and broth to bowl with scallops and shrimp; discard any unopened clams.

3. Heat remaining 3 teaspoons oil in same saucepan. Add onion and garlic; cook and stir 4 minutes or until tender. Add rice; cook and stir 2 minutes. Add remaining 3 cups broth, thyme and saffron; reduce heat to medium-low. Cover; simmer 15 minutes or until rice is tender. Stir in tomatoes, peas and parsley. Stir in seafood and reserved juices. Cover; remove from heat. Let stand 3 to 5 minutes or until seafood is hot.

makes 6 servings

NUTRIENTS PER SERVING

Calories:	395	Carbohydrate:	61g
Calories from Fat:	12%	Fiber:	3g
Total Fat:	5g	Protein:	24g
Saturated Fat:	1g	Sodium:	175mg
Cholesterol:	68mg		

Dietary Exchanges: 3½ Starch, 1 Vegetable, 2 Lean Meat

Oven-Roasted Boston Scrod

½ cup seasoned dry bread crumbs
1 teaspoon paprika
1 teaspoon grated fresh lemon peel
1 teaspoon dried dill weed
3 tablespoons all-purpose flour
2 egg whites
1 tablespoon water
1½ pounds Boston scrod or orange roughy fillets, cut into 6 (4-ounce) pieces
2 tablespoons margarine, melted
Tartar Sauce (recipe follows)
Lemon wedges

1. Preheat oven to 400°F. Spray 15×10-inch jelly-roll pan with nonstick cooking spray. Combine bread crumbs, paprika, lemon peel and dill in shallow bowl or pie plate. Place flour in resealable plastic food storage bag. Beat egg whites and water together in another shallow bowl or pie plate.

2. Add fish, one fillet at a time, to bag. Seal bag; turn to coat fish lightly. Dip fish into egg white mixture, letting excess drip off. Roll fish in bread crumb mixture. Place in prepared jelly-roll pan. Repeat with remaining fish fillets. Drizzle margarine evenly over fish. Bake 15 to 18 minutes or until fish begins to flake when tested with fork.

3. Prepare Tartar Sauce while fish is baking. Serve fish with lemon wedges and Tartar Sauce. *makes 6 servings*

Tartar Sauce

½ cup nonfat or reduced-fat mayonnaise
¼ cup sweet pickle relish
2 teaspoons Dijon mustard
¼ teaspoon hot pepper sauce (optional)

Combine all ingredients in small bowl; mix well.
makes ⅔ cup (6 servings)

NUTRIENTS PER SERVING

1 (4-ounce) piece fish plus about 1½ tablespoons tartar sauce = 1 serving

Calories:	215	Carbohydrate:	18g
Calories from Fat:	21%	Fiber:	<1g
Total Fat:	5g	Protein:	23g
Saturated Fat:	1g	Sodium:	754mg
Cholesterol:	49mg		

Dietary Exchanges: 1 Starch, 2½ Lean Meat

Pan Seared Halibut Steaks with Avocado Salsa

- 4 tablespoons chipotle salsa, divided
- ½ teaspoon salt, divided
- 4 small (4 to 5 ounces) or 2 large (8 to 10 ounces) halibut steaks, cut ¾ inch thick
- ½ cup diced tomato
- ½ ripe avocado, diced
- 2 tablespoons chopped cilantro
- Lime wedges (optional)

1. Combine 2 tablespoons salsa and ¼ teaspoon salt; spread over both sides of halibut.

2. Heat large nonstick skillet over medium heat until hot. Add halibut; cook 4 to 5 minutes per side or until fish is opaque in center.

3. Meanwhile, combine remaining 2 tablespoons salsa, ¼ teaspoon salt, tomato, avocado and cilantro in small bowl. Mix well and spoon over cooked fish. Garnish with lime wedges, if desired.

makes 4 servings

NUTRIENTS PER SERVING

Calories:	169	Carbohydrate:	2g
Calories from Fat:	36%	Fiber:	4g
Total Fat:	7g	Protein:	25g
Saturated Fat:	<1g	Sodium:	476mg
Cholesterol:	36mg		

Dietary Exchanges: 3 Lean Meat

Avocados are high in the "good" type of fat, monounsaturated fat. This type of fat has shown promise of lowering blood cholesterol levels when it is part of a diet low in saturated fat. Even "good" fat is high in calories, though, and should be eaten in moderation.

Cajun Catfish Skillet

- 2 cups water
- 1 cup uncooked rice*
- ¼ teaspoon salt
- ¼ teaspoon ground red pepper
- ¼ teaspoon ground white pepper
- ¼ teaspoon ground black pepper
- ½ cup minced green onions
- ½ cup minced green pepper
- ½ cup minced celery
- 2 cloves garlic, minced
- 1 tablespoon margarine
- 1 pound catfish nuggets or other firm flesh white fish**
- 1 can (15½ ounces) tomato sauce
- 1 teaspoon dried oregano leaves

**Recipe based on regular-milled long grain white rice.*

***Substitute 1 pound chicken nuggets for fish, if desired.*

Combine water, rice, salt, red pepper, white pepper, and black pepper in 3-quart saucepan. Bring to a boil; stir. Reduce heat; cover and simmer 15 minutes or until rice is tender and liquid is absorbed. Cook onions, green pepper, celery, and garlic in margarine in large skillet over medium-high heat until tender. Stir vegetable mixture, catfish nuggets, tomato sauce, and oregano into hot rice. Cover and cook over medium heat 7 to 8 minutes or until catfish flakes with fork. *makes 4 servings*

to microwave: Combine water, rice, salt, red pepper, white pepper, and black pepper in deep 2½- to 3-quart microproof baking dish. Cover and cook on HIGH 5 minutes. Reduce setting to MEDIUM (50% power) and cook 15 minutes or until rice is tender and liquid is absorbed. Combine onions, green pepper, celery, garlic, and margarine in 2-cup glass measure; cook on HIGH 2 minutes or until onions are tender. Stir vegetable mixture, catfish nuggets, tomato sauce, and oregano into hot rice. Cover and cook on HIGH 6 to 8 minutes, stirring after 3 minutes, or until catfish flakes with fork.

Favorite recipe from **USA Rice Federation**

NUTRIENTS PER SERVING

Calories:	351	Carbohydrate:	49g
Calories from Fat:	17%	Fiber:	3g
Total Fat:	7g	Protein:	24g
Saturated Fat:	2g	Sodium:	909mg
Cholesterol:	66mg		

Dietary Exchanges: 3 Starch, 1 Vegetable, 2 Lean Meat

Clam Chowder

- 1 can (5 ounces) whole baby clams, undrained
- 1 potato, peeled and coarsely chopped
- ¼ cup finely chopped onion
- ⅔ cup evaporated skimmed milk
- Pinch white pepper
- Pinch dried thyme leaves
- 1 tablespoon reduced-fat margarine
- Red pepper strip for garnish (optional)
- Greens for garnish (optional)

1. Drain clams; reserve juice. Add enough water to reserved juice to measure ⅔ cup. Combine clam juice mixture, potato and onion in large saucepan. Bring to a boil over high heat. Reduce heat to medium-low. Simmer 8 minutes or until potato is tender.

2. Add milk, pepper and thyme to saucepan. Increase heat to medium-high. Cook and stir 2 minutes. Add margarine. Cook 5 minutes or until soup thickens, stirring occasionally. Stir in clams. Cook 5 minutes or until clams are firm, stirring occasionally. Garnish with red pepper strip, thyme and greens, if desired. *makes 2 servings*

NUTRIENTS PER SERVING

Calories:	204	Carbohydrate:	30g
Calories from Fat:	17%	Fiber:	1g
Total Fat:	4g	Protein:	14g
Saturated Fat:	1g	Sodium:	205mg
Cholesterol:	47mg		

Dietary Exchanges: 1 Starch, 1 Milk, 1 Lean Meat

Tuna Salad Pita Pockets

- 1 (9-ounce) can tuna, drained
- 1 cup chopped cucumber
- ¼ cup part-skim ricotta cheese
- 2 tablespoons reduced-fat mayonnaise
- 2 tablespoons red wine vinegar
- 2 green onions, chopped
- 1 tablespoon sweet pickle relish
- 2 cloves garlic, finely chopped
- ½ teaspoon salt
- ¼ teaspoon black pepper
- 1 cup alfalfa sprouts
- 2 pita rounds, halved

Combine all ingredients except sprouts and pita halves. Fill pita halves with sprouts and tuna mixture.

makes 4 servings

NUTRIENTS PER SERVING

1 pita pocket = 1 serving

Calories:	209	Carbohydrate:	22g
Calories from Fat:	18%	Fiber:	<1g
Total Fat:	4g	Protein:	22g
Saturated Fat:	1g	Sodium:	752mg
Cholesterol:	22mg		

Dietary Exchanges: 1½ Starch, 2 Lean Meat

recipe tip

Ricotta resembles cottage cheese but is smoother, richer and creamier. It is prepared from whey left over from making mozzarella cheese. Like so many ingredients used in Italian cooking, it is inexpensive and readily available.

Mustard-Dill Salmon Steaks

- 1 can (10¾ ounces) reduced-fat cream of celery soup
- ½ cup fat-free (skim) milk
- ¼ cup finely chopped onion
- 2 teaspoons Dijon mustard
- 1 clove garlic, minced
- ¾ teaspoon dried dill weed
- 1 cup seedless red grapes, halved, divided
- 4 (6- to 8-ounce) boneless salmon steaks or fillets,* ¾ inch thick
- 2 tablespoons chopped fresh parsley

***Halibut, swordfish or tuna may be substituted for salmon. Nutritionals will vary.*

Preheat oven to 350°F. Combine soup, milk, onion, mustard, garlic and dill in small bowl; mix well. Spread half of soup mixture and half of grapes in 13×9-inch baking dish. Place fish over soup mixture. Pour remaining soup mixture over fish and sprinkle with remaining grapes.

Bake 20 to 25 minutes or until fish begins to flake when tested with fork. Sprinkle with parsley.

makes 4 servings

NUTRIENTS PER SERVING

Calories:	275	Carbohydrate:	14g
Calories from Fat:	26%	Fiber:	1g
Total Fat:	8g	Protein:	35g
Saturated Fat:	2g	Sodium:	713mg
Cholesterol:	89mg		

Dietary Exchanges: 1 Starch, 4 Lean Meat

Tip

Salmon has a higher fat content than most fish, but the fat is made up primarily of omega-3 fatty acids. There is a wealth of research available today that links consumption of omega-3 fatty acids with the reduced risk of heart attack and heart disease.

Linguine with Red Clam Sauce

- Nonstick cooking spray
- 1 onion, finely chopped
- 2 cloves garlic, minced
- 2 tablespoons finely chopped fresh parsley
- 2 teaspoons dried oregano leaves
- 1 can (14 ounces) Italian plum tomatoes, undrained, coarsely chopped
- 1 can (8 ounces) reduced-sodium tomato sauce
- 2 cans (7½ ounces each) baby clams, undrained
- 1 tablespoon lemon juice
- Salt and black pepper
- 8 ounces linguine, cooked and kept warm

1. Spray large saucepan with cooking spray. Heat over medium heat until hot. Add onion and garlic; cook and stir about 3 minutes or until tender. Stir in parsley and oregano; cook 1 to 2 minutes.

2. Add tomatoes with liquid and tomato sauce to saucepan; bring to a boil. Reduce heat and simmer, uncovered, about 10 minutes or until mixture is of medium sauce consistency. Stir in clams and lemon juice; cook about 3 minutes or until heated through. Season to taste with salt and pepper.

3. Spoon sauce over linguine in large bowl and toss.

makes 4 servings

NUTRIENTS PER SERVING

Calories:	431	Carbohydrate:	61g
Calories from Fat:	7%	Fiber:	2g
Total Fat:	3g	Protein:	37g
Saturated Fat:	<1g	Sodium:	300mg
Cholesterol:	71mg		

Dietary Exchanges: 3 Starch, 2 Vegetable, 3 Lean Meat

Grilled Swordfish with Pineapple Salsa

1 tablespoon lime juice
2 cloves garlic, minced
4 swordfish steaks (5 ounces each)
½ teaspoon chili powder or black pepper
Pineapple Salsa (recipe follows)

1. Combine lime juice and garlic on plate. Dip swordfish in juice; sprinkle with chili powder.

2. Spray cold grid with nonstick cooking spray. Adjust grid 4 to 6 inches above heat. Preheat grill to medium-high heat. Grill fish, covered, 2 to 3 minutes. Turn over; grill 1 to 2 minutes more or until just opaque in center and still very moist. Top each serving with about 3 tablespoons Pineapple Salsa. *makes 4 servings*

Pineapple Salsa

½ cup finely chopped fresh pineapple
¼ cup finely chopped red bell pepper
1 green onion, thinly sliced
2 tablespoons lime juice
½ jalapeño pepper,* seeded and minced
1 tablespoon chopped fresh cilantro or fresh basil

**Jalapeño peppers can sting and irritate the skin; wear rubber gloves when handling peppers and do not touch eyes. Wash hands after handling peppers.*

Combine all ingredients in small nonmetallic bowl. Serve at room temperature. *makes 4 servings*

NUTRIENTS PER SERVING

1 (5-ounce) steak plus 3 tablespoons salsa = 1 serving

Calories:	194	Carbohydrate:	6g
Calories from Fat:	28%	Fiber:	1g
Total Fat:	6g	Protein:	28g
Saturated Fat:	2g	Sodium:	183mg
Cholesterol:	56mg		

Dietary Exchanges: ½ Fruit, 3 Lean Meat

Fettuccine with Shrimp in Light Tomato Sauce

- 1 tablespoon olive or vegetable oil
- 1 pound medium shrimp, peeled and deveined
- 3 cloves garlic, finely chopped
- 1 jar (26 to 28 ounces) RAGÚ® Light Pasta Sauce
- ⅛ teaspoon red pepper flakes
- 1 package (12 ounces) fettuccine, cooked and drained
- 2 tablespoons grated Parmesan cheese

In 10-inch skillet, heat oil over medium heat and cook shrimp and garlic 3 minutes or until shrimp are almost pink. Stir in pasta sauce and red pepper flakes. Simmer uncovered, stirring occasionally, 2 minutes or until shrimp turn pink and sauce is heated through. Spoon sauce and shrimp over hot fettuccine and sprinkle with cheese. Garnish, if desired, with finely chopped fresh parsley. *makes 6 servings*

NUTRIENTS PER SERVING

Calories:	297	Carbohydrate:	41g
Calories from Fat:	16%	Fiber:	2g
Total Fat:	5g	Protein:	21g
Saturated Fat:	1g	Sodium:	554mg
Cholesterol:	127mg		

Dietary Exchanges: 2 Starch, 2 Vegetable, 1 Lean Meat, ½ Fat

recipe tip

Peel shrimp by gently pulling the legs from the shell. Then, loosen the shell with your fingers and slide it off. Devein shrimp by first making a small cut along the back. Then, lift out the dark vein with the tip of a knife. You might find deveining easier if you do it under cold running water.

Baked Orange Roughy with Sautéed Vegetables

- 2 orange roughy fillets (about 4 ounces each)
- 2 teaspoons olive oil
- 1 medium carrot, cut into matchstick pieces
- 4 medium mushrooms, sliced
- ⅓ cup chopped onion
- ¼ cup chopped green or yellow bell pepper
- 1 clove garlic, minced
- Black pepper
- Lemon wedges

1. Preheat oven to 350°F. Place fish fillets in shallow baking dish. Bake 15 minutes or until fish flakes easily when tested with fork.

2. Heat olive oil in small nonstick skillet over medium-high heat. Add carrot; cook 3 minutes, stirring occasionally. Add mushrooms, onion, bell pepper and garlic; cook and stir 2 minutes or until vegetables are crisp-tender.

3. Place fish on serving plates; top with vegetable mixture. Sprinkle with black pepper. Serve with lemon wedges.

makes 2 servings

to microwave: Place fish in shallow microwavable dish. Microwave, covered, on HIGH 2 minutes or until fish flakes easily when tested with fork.

to broil: Place fish on rack of broiler pan. Broil 4 to 6 inches from heat 4 minutes on each side or until fish flakes easily when tested with fork.

NUTRIENTS PER SERVING

Calories:	157	Carbohydrate:	10g
Calories from Fat:	32%	Fiber:	3g
Total Fat:	6g	Protein:	18g
Saturated Fat:	1g	Sodium:	84mg
Cholesterol:	22mg		

Dietary Exchanges: 1½ Vegetable, 2 Lean Meat

Grilled Spiced Halibut, Pineapple and Pepper Skewers

- 2 tablespoons lemon juice or lime juice
- 1 teaspoon chili powder
- 1 teaspoon minced garlic
- ½ teaspoon ground cumin
- ¼ teaspoon ground cinnamon
- ⅛ teaspoon ground cloves
- ½ pound boneless skinless halibut steak, about 1 inch thick
- ½ small pineapple, peeled, halved lengthwise and cut into 24 pieces
- 1 large green or red bell pepper, cut into 24 squares

1. Combine lemon juice, chili powder, garlic, cumin, cinnamon and cloves in large resealable plastic food storage bag; knead until blended.

2. Rinse fish and pat dry. Cut into 12 cubes about 1 to 1¼ inches square. Add fish to bag; press out air and seal. Turn bag gently to coat fish with marinade. Refrigerate halibut 30 minutes to 1 hour. Soak 12 (6- to 8-inch) bamboo skewers in water while fish marinates.

3. Alternately thread 2 pieces pineapple, 2 pieces pepper and 1 piece fish onto each skewer.

4. Spray cold grid with nonstick cooking spray. Adjust grid 4 to 6 inches above heat. Preheat grill to medium-high heat. Place skewers on grill, cover if possible (or tent with foil) and grill 3 to 4 minutes or until grill marks appear on bottoms. Turn and grill skewers 3 to 4 minutes or until fish is opaque and flakes easily when tested with fork.

makes 6 servings

NUTRIENTS PER SERVING

2 skewers = 1 serving

Calories:	84	Carbohydrate:	11g
Calories from Fat:	13%	Fiber:	1g
Total Fat:	1g	Protein:	8g
Saturated Fat:	<1g	Sodium:	23mg
Cholesterol:	12mg		

Dietary Exchanges: ½ Fruit, 1 Lean Meat

Beijing Fillet of Sole

- 2 tablespoons reduced-sodium soy sauce
- 2 teaspoons dark sesame oil
- 4 sole fillets (6 ounces each)
- 1¼ cups preshredded cabbage or coleslaw mix
- ½ cup crushed chow mein noodles
- 1 egg white, slightly beaten
- 2 teaspoons sesame seeds
- 1 package (10 ounces) frozen snow peas, cooked and drained

1. Heat oven to 350°F. Combine soy sauce and oil in small bowl. Place sole in shallow dish. Lightly brush both sides of sole with soy mixture.

2. Combine cabbage, crushed noodles, egg white and remaining soy mixture in small bowl. Spoon evenly over sole. Roll up each fillet and place, seam side down, in shallow foil-lined roasting pan.

3. Sprinkle rolls with sesame seeds. Bake 25 to 30 minutes or until fish flakes when tested with fork. Serve with snow peas. *makes 4 servings*

NUTRIENTS PER SERVING

Calories:	252	Carbohydrate:	6g
Calories from Fat:	29%	Fiber:	<1g
Total Fat:	8g	Protein:	34g
Saturated Fat:	1g	Sodium:	435mg
Cholesterol:	80mg		

Dietary Exchanges: 1½ Vegetable, 4 Lean Meat

Scallops and Marinara Sauce on Spinach Fettuccine

- 3 teaspoons olive oil, divided
- 1 cup chopped onion
- 1 cup sliced mushrooms
- 1 red bell pepper, chopped
- 1 can (14½ ounces) Italian-style stewed tomatoes, undrained
- ½ teaspoon Thai chili paste* (optional)
- 9 ounces fresh uncooked spinach fettuccine
- 12 ounces scallops, rinsed and drained
- 2 tablespoons freshly grated Parmesan cheese
- 2 teaspoons snipped chives

**Thai chili paste is available at some larger supermarkets and at Oriental markets.*

1. For marinara sauce, heat 1 teaspoon olive oil in saucepan over medium heat until hot. Add onion. Cook and stir 3 minutes or until onion is soft. Add mushrooms, bell pepper, tomatoes and chili paste. Bring to a boil over high heat. Reduce heat to low. Cover and simmer 15 minutes, stirring occasionally.

2. Cook fettuccine according to package directions, omitting salt. Drain; keep warm. Meanwhile, heat remaining 2 teaspoons olive oil in large nonstick skillet over medium heat until hot. Add scallops. Cook and stir 4 minutes or until scallops are opaque.

3. Divide spinach fettuccine among serving plates. Top with marinara sauce and scallops. Sprinkle with Parmesan and chives. *makes 4 servings*

Prep and Cook Time: 30 minutes

NUTRIENTS PER SERVING

Calories:	350	Carbohydrate:	48g
Calories from Fat:	19%	Fiber:	2g
Total Fat:	8g	Protein:	24g
Saturated Fat:	1g	Sodium:	470mg
Cholesterol:	42mg		

Dietary Exchanges: 2 Starch, 1½ Vegetable, 3 Lean Meat

Blackened Catfish with Easy Tartar Sauce and Rice

Easy Tartar Sauce (recipe follows)
4 (4-ounce) catfish fillets
2 teaspoons lemon juice
Nonstick garlic-flavored cooking spray
2 teaspoons blackened or Cajun seasoning blend
1 cup hot cooked rice

1. Prepare Easy Tartar Sauce.

2. Rinse catfish under cold running water; pat dry with paper towel. Sprinkle fillets with 2 teaspoons lemon juice; coat with cooking spray. Sprinkle with seasoning blend; coat again with cooking spray.

3. Heat large nonstick skillet over medium-high heat until hot. Add 2 fillets to skillet, seasoned side down. Cook 3 minutes. Reduce heat to medium; cook 3 minutes more or until fish begins to flake when tested with fork. Remove fillets from skillet; keep warm. Repeat with remaining fillets. Serve with Easy Tartar Sauce and rice.

makes 4 servings

Easy Tartar Sauce

¼ cup fat-free or reduced-fat mayonnaise
2 tablespoons sweet pickle relish
1 teaspoon lemon juice

Combine mayonnaise, relish and 1 teaspoon lemon juice in small bowl; mix well. Refrigerate until ready to serve.

makes about ¼ cup

NUTRIENTS PER SERVING

1 fillet plus about 1 tablespoon tartar sauce plus ¼ cup rice = 1 serving

Calories:	290	Carbohydrate:	33g
Calories from Fat:	26%	Fiber:	1g
Total Fat:	8g	Protein:	19g
Saturated Fat:	2g	Sodium:	344mg
Cholesterol:	54mg		

Dietary Exchanges: 2 Starch, 2 Lean Meat, 1 Fat

Poached Salmon with Tarragon Sauce

1 cup defatted low-sodium chicken broth*
¼ cup lemon juice
1 bay leaf
⅛ teaspoon black pepper
4 fresh or thawed frozen pink salmon steaks (5 ounces each), cut ¾ inch thick
⅓ cup plain nonfat yogurt
¼ cup fat-free mayonnaise
2 tablespoons thinly sliced green onion
2 tablespoons chopped fresh parsley
1 teaspoon chopped fresh tarragon *or* ¼ teaspoon dried tarragon leaves, crushed

**To defat chicken broth, skim fat off surface of broth with spoon. Or, place can of broth in refrigerator at least 2 hours ahead of time. Before using, remove fat that has hardened on surface of broth.*

Combine chicken broth, lemon juice, bay leaf and pepper in large skillet. Bring to a boil over high heat. Carefully place salmon steaks in skillet; return to a boil. Immediately reduce heat to medium-low. Simmer, covered, 8 to 10 minutes or until salmon begins to flake when tested with a fork. Remove salmon from skillet.

Meanwhile, combine yogurt, mayonnaise, green onion, parsley and tarragon in small bowl. Refrigerate, covered, until ready to serve. Spoon sauce over salmon. Salmon may be served chilled. *makes 4 servings*

NUTRIENTS PER SERVING

Calories:	233	Carbohydrate:	20g
Calories from Fat:	23%	Fiber:	<1g
Total Fat:	6g	Protein:	25g
Saturated Fat:	1g	Sodium:	527mg
Cholesterol:	26mg		

Dietary Exchanges: 1½ Starch, 3 Lean Meat

recipe tip

Use two slotted metal spatulas to carefully remove poached fish from the pan. Poached fish is delicate and tends to break apart easily.

Veggie Tuna Pasta

1 package (16 ounces) medium pasta shells
1 bag (16 ounces) BIRDS EYE® frozen Farm Fresh Mixtures Broccoli, Corn & Red Peppers
1 can (10 ounces) chunky light tuna, packed in water
1 can (10¾ ounces) reduced-fat cream of mushroom soup

• In large saucepan, cook pasta according to package directions. Add vegetables during last 10 minutes; drain and return to saucepan.

• Stir in tuna and soup. Add salt and pepper to taste.* Cook over medium heat until heated through.

makes 4 servings

**Nutritionals will vary.*

serving suggestion: For a creamier dish, add a few tablespoons water; blend well.

Prep Time: 2 minutes
Cook Time: 12 to 15 minutes

NUTRIENTS PER SERVING

Calories:	626	Carbohydrate:	110g
Calories from Fat:	4%	Fiber:	6g
Total Fat:	3g	Protein:	37g
Saturated Fat:	<1g	Sodium:	567mg
Cholesterol:	23mg		

Dietary Exchanges: 7 Starch, 1 Vegetable, 2 Lean Meat

Herbed Scallops and Shrimp

- ¼ cup chopped fresh parsley
- ¼ cup lime juice
- 2 tablespoons chopped fresh mint
- 2 tablespoons chopped fresh rosemary
- 1 tablespoon olive oil
- 1 tablespoon honey
- 2 cloves garlic, minced
- ¼ teaspoon black pepper
- ½ pound raw jumbo shrimp, peeled and deveined
- ½ pound bay or halved sea scallops
- Lime slices (optional)
- Fresh mint sprigs (optional)

1. Preheat broiler. Combine parsley, lime juice, mint, rosemary, oil, honey, garlic and black pepper in medium bowl; blend well. Add shrimp and scallops. Cover; refrigerate 1 hour.

2. Arrange shrimp and scallops on skewers. Place on broiler pan. Brush with marinade. Broil 5 to 6 minutes or until shrimp are opaque and scallops are lightly browned. Serve immediately with lime slices and fresh mint sprigs, if desired. *makes 4 servings*

NUTRIENTS PER SERVING

Calories:	152	Carbohydrate:	8g
Calories from Fat:	27%	Fiber:	0g
Total Fat:	5g	Protein:	20g
Saturated Fat:	1g	Sodium:	223mg
Cholesterol:	111mg		

Dietary Exchanges: 1 Vegetable, 2½ Lean Meat

recipe tip

Bay scallops are tiny scallops harvested mainly from the East Coast. Sea scallops are about three times as large as bay scallops and tend to cost less by weight. Cut sea scallops into halves or thirds for an economical alternative to bay scallops.

Latin-Style Pasta & Beans

8 ounces uncooked mostaccioli, penne or bow tie pasta
1 tablespoon olive oil
1 medium onion, chopped
1 yellow or red bell pepper, diced
4 cloves garlic, minced
1 can (15 ounces) red or black beans, rinsed and drained
¾ cup canned vegetable broth
¾ cup medium-hot salsa or picante sauce
2 teaspoons ground cumin
⅓ cup coarsely chopped fresh cilantro
Lime wedges

1. Cook pasta according to package directions, omitting salt. Drain; set aside.

2. Meanwhile, heat oil in large skillet over medium heat. Add onion; cook 5 minutes, stirring occasionally. Add bell pepper and garlic; cook 3 minutes, stirring occasionally. Add beans, vegetable broth, salsa and cumin; simmer, uncovered, 5 minutes.

3. Add pasta to skillet; cook 1 minute, tossing frequently. Stir in cilantro; spoon onto 4 plates. Serve with lime wedges. *makes 4 servings*

NUTRIENTS PER SERVING

Calories:	390	Carbohydrate:	74g
Calories from Fat:	12%	Fiber:	8g
Total Fat:	6g	Protein:	18g
Saturated Fat:	1g	Sodium:	557mg
Cholesterol:	0mg		

Dietary Exchanges: 4 Starch, 1 Vegetable, ½ Fat

Spinach Lasagna

- 5 lasagna noodles
- Nonstick cooking spray
- 2 cups sliced fresh mushrooms
- 1 cup chopped onion
- 1 cup chopped green bell pepper
- 2 cloves garlic, minced
- 2 cans (8 ounces each) no-salt-added tomato sauce
- 1 teaspoon chopped fresh basil *or* ¼ teaspoon dried basil leaves, crushed
- 1 teaspoon chopped fresh oregano *or* ¼ teaspoon dried oregano leaves, crushed
- ¼ teaspoon ground red pepper
- 2 egg whites
- 1½ cups 1% low-fat cottage cheese or light ricotta cheese
- ¼ cup grated Romano or Parmesan cheese
- 3 tablespoons fine dry bread crumbs
- 1 package (10 ounces) frozen chopped spinach, thawed and well drained
- ¾ cup (3 ounces) shredded part-skim mozzarella cheese
- ¼ cup chopped fresh parsley

Prepare noodles according to package directions, omitting salt; drain. Rinse under cold water; drain.

Coat large skillet with cooking spray. Add mushrooms, onion, bell pepper and garlic; cook and stir over medium heat until vegetables are tender. Stir in tomato sauce, basil, oregano and red pepper. Bring to a boil over medium-high heat. Reduce heat to medium-low. Simmer, uncovered, 10 minutes, stirring occasionally.

Preheat oven to 350°F. Combine egg whites, cottage cheese, Romano cheese and bread crumbs in medium bowl. Stir spinach into cottage cheese mixture. Cut noodles in half crosswise. Spread ½ cup sauce in ungreased 8- or 9-inch square baking dish. Top with half the noodles, half the spinach mixture and half the remaining sauce. Repeat layers.

Cover and bake 45 minutes or until heated through. Sprinkle with mozzarella cheese. Bake, uncovered, 2 to 3 minutes or until cheese melts. Sprinkle with parsley. Let stand 10 minutes before serving. *makes 4 servings*

NUTRIENTS PER SERVING

Calories:	350	Carbohydrate:	40g
Calories from Fat:	21%	Fiber:	7g
Total Fat:	8g	Protein:	30g
Saturated Fat:	4g	Sodium:	746mg
Cholesterol:	23mg		

Dietary Exchanges: 1 Starch, 5 Vegetable, 2½ Lean Meat, ½ Fat

Pasta with Spinach-Cheese Sauce

- ¼ cup FILIPPO BERIO® Extra-Virgin Olive Oil, divided
- 1 medium onion, chopped
- 1 clove garlic, chopped
- 3 cups chopped fresh spinach, washed and well drained
- 1 cup low-fat ricotta or cottage cheese
- ½ cup chopped fresh parsley
- 1 teaspoon dried basil leaves
- 1 teaspoon lemon juice
- ¼ teaspoon black pepper
- ¼ teaspoon ground nutmeg
- ¾ pound uncooked spaghetti

1. Heat 3 tablespoons olive oil in large skillet over medium heat. Sauté onion and garlic until onion is tender.

2. Add spinach to skillet; cook 3 to 5 minutes or until spinach wilts.

3. Place spinach mixture, cheese, parsley, basil, lemon juice, pepper and nutmeg in covered blender container. Blend until smooth. Leave in blender, covered, to keep sauce warm.

4. Cook pasta according to package directions. Do not overcook. Drain pasta, reserving ¼ cup water. In large bowl, toss pasta with remaining 1 tablespoon olive oil.

5. Add reserved ¼ cup water to sauce in blender. Blend; serve over pasta.

makes 4 servings

NUTRIENTS PER SERVING

Calories:	584	Carbohydrate:	83g
Calories from Fat:	27%	Fiber:	7g
Total Fat:	17g	Protein:	24g
Saturated Fat:	3g	Sodium:	139mg
Cholesterol:	11mg		

Dietary Exchanges: 4½ Starch, 2 Vegetable, 1 Lean Meat, 3 Fat

Spaghetti Squash Primavera

- 2 teaspoons vegetable oil
- ½ teaspoon finely chopped garlic
- ¼ cup finely chopped red onion
- ¼ cup thinly sliced carrot
- ¼ cup thinly sliced red bell pepper
- ¼ cup thinly sliced green bell pepper
- 1 can (14½ ounces) Italian-style stewed tomatoes, undrained
- ½ cup thinly sliced yellow squash
- ½ cup thinly sliced zucchini
- ½ cup frozen whole kernel corn, thawed
- ½ teaspoon dried oregano leaves
- ⅛ teaspoon dried thyme leaves
- 1 spaghetti squash (about 2 pounds)
- 4 teaspoons grated Parmesan cheese (optional)
- 2 tablespoons finely chopped fresh parsley

1. Heat oil in large skillet over medium-high heat until hot. Add garlic. Cook and stir 3 minutes. Add onion, carrot and peppers. Cook and stir 3 minutes. Add tomatoes, yellow squash, zucchini, corn, oregano and thyme. Cook 5 minutes or until heated through, stirring occasionally.

2. Cut spaghetti squash lengthwise in half. Remove seeds. Cover with plastic wrap. Microwave at HIGH 9 minutes or until squash separates easily into strands when tested with fork.

3. Cut each squash half lengthwise into halves; separate strands with fork. Spoon vegetables evenly over squash. Top servings evenly with cheese, if desired, and parsley before serving.

makes 4 servings

NUTRIENTS PER SERVING

Calories:	101	Carbohydrate:	18g
Calories from Fat:	25%	Fiber:	5g
Total Fat:	3g	Protein:	3g
Saturated Fat:	<1g	Sodium:	11mg
Cholesterol:	0mg		

Dietary Exchanges: 1 Starch, 1 Vegetable, ½ Fat

Bean and Vegetable Egg Rolls

Plum Dipping Sauce (recipe follows)
1 tablespoon sesame seeds
1 tablespoon dark sesame oil
2 green onions with tops, sliced
1 tablespoon minced fresh ginger
2 cloves garlic, minced
2 cups shredded napa cabbage
1 cup shredded carrots
½ cup chopped celery
½ cup chopped mushrooms
4 ounces fresh or canned bean sprouts, rinsed
1 can (15 ounces) chick-peas, rinsed and drained
1½ teaspoons reduced-sodium soy sauce
Pepper (optional)
1 egg, beaten
12 egg roll wrappers
Peanut or vegetable oil

1. Prepare Plum Dipping Sauce.

2. Combine sesame seeds and sesame oil in large skillet. Cook and stir over low heat 2 to 3 minutes or until sesame seeds begin to brown. Add green onions, ginger and garlic; cook and stir 1 to 2 minutes. Add cabbage, carrots, celery, mushrooms and bean sprouts; cover. Cook 8 minutes or until cabbage is wilted. Stir in chick-peas and soy sauce; season to taste with pepper, if desired. Cool 10 minutes; stir in egg.

3. Place ⅓ cup vegetable mixture near one corner of egg roll wrapper. Brush edges of egg roll wrapper with water. Fold bottom corner of egg roll wrapper up over filling; fold sides in and roll up. Repeat with remaining filling and egg roll wrappers.

4. Heat 1 inch peanut oil in large heavy saucepan over medium-high heat until oil is 375°F; adjust heat to maintain temperature. Fry egg rolls 3 to 5 minutes or until golden. Garnish, if desired. *makes 12 servings*

Plum Dipping Sauce

⅔ cup plum sauce
3 tablespoons reduced-sodium soy sauce
2 tablespoons rice wine vinegar or cider vinegar
1 tablespoon grated fresh ginger
1 tablespoon honey
2 green onions with tops, sliced
3 to 4 drops hot chili oil (optional)

Combine all ingredients in medium bowl; mix well. Cover; refrigerate until ready to serve. *makes about 1 cup*

continued on page 202

Bean and Vegetable Egg Roll

Bean and Vegetable Egg Rolls, continued

note: While preparing egg rolls, cover remaining egg roll wrappers with a damp towel to prevent drying out.

NUTRIENTS PER SERVING

1 egg roll plus 1⅓ tablespoons sauce = 1 serving

Calories:	118	Carbohydrate:	20g
Calories from Fat:	20%	Fiber:	3g
Total Fat:	3g	Protein:	5g
Saturated Fat:	<1g	Sodium:	335mg
Cholesterol:	18mg		

Dietary Exchanges: 1 Starch, 1 Vegetable, ½ Fat

Linguine with Fresh Tomato Basil Sauce

- 1 cup chopped onion
- 3 cloves garlic, minced
- ¼ teaspoon ground black pepper
- 2 tablespoons FLEISCHMANN'S® Original Margarine
- 2 cups sliced mushrooms
- 3 large tomatoes, peeled, seeded and chopped
- 1 tablespoon dried basil leaves, crushed, *or* ¼ cup chopped fresh basil leaves
- 1 teaspoon sugar
- 12 ounces uncooked linguine, cooked according to package directions in unsalted water and drained

In large skillet, over medium-high heat, cook and stir onion, garlic and pepper in margarine until onion is tender, about 3 minutes. Add mushrooms; cook 5 minutes. Add tomatoes, basil and sugar; heat to a boil. Reduce heat to low; simmer, uncovered, 15 to 20 minutes. Serve over linguine.

makes 6 servings

NUTRIENTS PER SERVING

Calories:	220	Carbohydrate:	40g
Calories from Fat:	19%	Fiber:	3g
Total Fat:	5g	Protein:	7g
Saturated Fat:	1g	Sodium:	142mg
Cholesterol:	0mg		

Dietary Exchanges: 2 Starch, 1 Vegetable, 1 Fat

Vegetarian Fried Rice

- 4 dried mushrooms
- 4 cups cooked long-grain rice
- 3 eggs
- ¾ teaspoon salt, divided
- 2½ tablespoons vegetable oil, divided
- 1 teaspoon minced fresh ginger
- 1 clove garlic, minced
- 3 green onions with tops, thinly sliced
- 4 ounces bean curd, cut into ¼-inch cubes and deep-fried
- 1 tablespoon soy sauce
- ¼ teaspoon sugar
- 1 cup bean sprouts, coarsely chopped
- ½ cup thawed frozen peas

1. Place mushrooms in small bowl; cover with hot water. Let stand 30 minutes; drain, reserving liquid. Squeeze out excess water. Remove stems; discard. Chop caps.

2. Rub rice with wet hands so all the grains are separated.

3. Beat eggs with ¼ teaspoon salt in medium bowl. Heat ½ tablespoon oil in wok or large skillet over medium heat. Add eggs; cook and stir until soft curds form.

4. Remove wok from heat; cut eggs into small pieces with spoon. Remove from wok; set aside.

5. Heat remaining 2 tablespoons oil in wok over high heat. Add ginger, garlic and onions; stir-fry 10 seconds. Add mushrooms, ¼ cup reserved mushroom liquid, bean curd, soy sauce and sugar. Cook until most of the liquid evaporates, about 4 minutes. Add bean sprouts and peas; cook 30 seconds.

6. Stir in rice and remaining ½ teaspoon salt; heat thoroughly. Stir in eggs just before serving.

makes 4 servings

NUTRIENTS PER SERVING

Calories:	396	Carbohydrate:	54g
Calories from Fat:	31%	Fiber:	3g
Total Fat:	14g	Protein:	14g
Saturated Fat:	3g	Sodium:	770mg
Cholesterol:	159mg		

Dietary Exchanges: 3½ Starch, 2 Vegetable, 2½ Fat

Middle Eastern Grilled Vegetable Wraps

- 1 large eggplant (about 1 pound), cut crosswise into ⅜-inch slices
- Nonstick cooking spray
- ¾ pound large mushrooms
- 1 red bell pepper, seeded, cored and quartered
- 1 green bell pepper, seeded, cored and quartered
- 2 green onions, sliced
- ¼ cup fresh lemon juice
- ⅛ teaspoon black pepper
- 4 large (10-inch) fat-free flour tortillas
- ½ cup (4 ounces) hummus (chick-pea spread)*
- ⅓ cup lightly packed fresh cilantro
- 12 large fresh basil leaves
- 12 large fresh mint leaves

**Four ounces crumbled reduced-fat feta cheese may be substituted for hummus.*

1. Prepare barbecue grill for direct cooking.

2. Lightly spray eggplant with cooking spray. If mushrooms are small, thread onto skewers.

3. Grill bell peppers, skin side down, over hot coals until blackened. Place in paper bag; seal. Steam 5 minutes; remove skin. Grill eggplant and mushrooms, covered, over medium coals about 2 minutes on each side or until tender and lightly browned. Cut eggplant and bell peppers into ½-inch strips; cut mushrooms into quarters. Combine vegetables, onions, lemon juice and black pepper in medium bowl.

4. Grill tortillas on both sides about 1 minute or until warmed. Spoon ¼ of hummus, ¼ of herbs, and ¼ of vegetables down center of each tortilla. Roll to enclose filling; serve immediately. *makes 4 servings*

NUTRIENTS PER SERVING

1 wrap = 1 serving

Calories:	234	Carbohydrate:	41g
Calories from Fat:	21%	Fiber:	14g
Total Fat:	6g	Protein:	8g
Saturated Fat:	1g	Sodium:	340mg
Cholesterol:	0mg		

Dietary Exchanges: 2 Starch, 2 Vegetable, 1 Fat

Tofu Stir-Fry

- 2 cups uncooked instant rice
- 2 teaspoons vegetable oil
- 2 cups broccoli florets
- 1 large carrot, sliced
- ½ green bell pepper, sliced
- ¼ cup frozen chopped onion
- ½ cup teriyaki sauce
- ½ cup orange juice
- 1 tablespoon cornstarch
- 1 teaspoon bottled minced garlic
- ½ teaspoon ground ginger
- ¼ to ½ teaspoon hot pepper sauce
- 1 package (10½ ounces) reduced-fat firm tofu, drained and cubed

1. Cook rice according to package directions.

2. While rice is cooking, heat oil in large skillet. Add broccoli, carrot, bell pepper and onion; cook and stir 3 minutes.

3. Combine teriyaki sauce, orange juice, cornstarch, garlic, ginger and pepper sauce in small bowl; mix well. Pour sauce over vegetables in skillet. Bring to a boil; cook and stir 1 minute.

4. Add tofu to skillet; stir gently to coat with sauce. Serve over rice. *makes 4 servings*

serving suggestion: For a special touch, garnish with red bell pepper strips.

NUTRIENTS PER SERVING

Calories:	354	Carbohydrate:	60g
Calories from Fat:	15%	Fiber:	5g
Total Fat:	6g	Protein:	16g
Saturated Fat:	<1g	Sodium:	1407mg
Cholesterol:	0mg		

Dietary Exchanges: 3 Starch, 2 Vegetable, 1 Lean Meat, ½ Fat

Veggie Kabobs with Tex-Mex Polenta

POLENTA

2¾ cups water
¾ cup yellow cornmeal
½ teaspoon salt
1 can (4 ounces) chopped green chilies, drained
½ cup (2 ounces) shredded Monterey Jack cheese
2 tablespoons shredded Cheddar cheese
2 tablespoons grated Parmesan cheese

VEGGIE KABOBS

½ cup olive oil
¼ cup cider vinegar
1 teaspoon salt
¾ teaspoon garlic powder
½ teaspoon black pepper
3 large bell peppers, cut into 1½-inch pieces
1 medium red onion, cut into 1-inch wedges
8 ounces fresh mushrooms

1. Combine water, cornmeal and salt in large microwavable bowl. Cover tightly; microwave at HIGH 10 to 12 minutes, stirring halfway through cooking time. Stir in chilies and Monterey Jack cheese. Cover; let stand 2 minutes. Grease 9-inch casserole. Spread cornmeal mixture into prepared casserole. Cover; refrigerate 2 hours or until firm.

2. Preheat broiler. Turn polenta out of casserole; cut into 6 wedges. Grease small baking sheet. Place polenta on baking sheet. Broil 6 inches from heat 5 to 6 minutes per side. Sprinkle with Cheddar and Parmesan cheeses.

3. Soak 8 to 10 wooden skewers in water. Combine oil, vinegar, salt, garlic powder and black pepper in medium bowl. Alternately thread bell peppers, onion and mushrooms onto skewers. Arrange skewers in shallow pan. Pour oil marinade over skewers. Cover; refrigerate at least 2 hours or overnight.

4. To complete recipe, preheat broiler. Transfer skewers to large baking sheet. Broil 8 to 10 minutes or until vegetables begin to brown. Serve with polenta. Garnish as desired. *makes 4 to 6 servings*

Make-Ahead Time: 2 hours to 1 day before serving
Final Prep and Cook Time: 30 minutes

NUTRIENTS PER SERVING

Calories:	195	Carbohydrate:	28g
Calories from Fat:	23%	Fiber:	5g
Total Fat:	5g	Protein:	11g
Saturated Fat:	3g	Sodium:	738mg
Cholesterol:	15mg		

Dietary Exchanges: 1 Starch, 3 Vegetable, 1 Lean Meat, 1 Fat

Grilled Portobello Mushroom Sandwich

1 large portobello mushroom cap, cleaned and stem removed
¼ medium green bell pepper, halved
1 thin slice red onion
1 whole wheat hamburger bun, split
2 tablespoons fat-free Italian dressing
1 (1-ounce) reduced-fat part-skim mozzarella cheese slice, cut in half (optional)

1. Brush mushroom, bell pepper, onion and cut sides of bun with some dressing; place vegetables over medium-hot coals. Grill 2 minutes.

2. Turn vegetables over; brush with dressing. Grill 2 minutes or until vegetables are tender. Remove bell pepper and onion from grill.

3. Place bun halves on grill. Turn mushroom, top side up; brush with any remaining dressing and cover with cheese, if desired. Grill 1 minute or until cheese is melted and bun is lightly toasted.

4. Cut bell pepper into strips. Place mushroom on bottom half of bun; top with pepper strips and onion slice. Cover with top half of bun. *makes 1 serving*

variation: To broil, brush mushroom, bell pepper, onion and cut sides of bun with dressing. Place vegetables on greased rack of broiler pan; set bun aside. Broil vegetables 4 to 6 inches from heat 3 minutes; turn over. Brush with dressing. Broil 3 minutes or until vegetables are tender. Place mushroom, top side up, on broiler pan; top with cheese, if desired. Place bun, cut sides up, on broiler pan. Broil 1 minute or until cheese is melted and bun is toasted. Assemble sandwich as directed above.

NUTRIENTS PER SERVING

1 sandwich = 1 serving

Calories:	225	Carbohydrate:	30g
Calories from Fat:	22%	Fiber:	6g
Total Fat:	6g	Protein:	15g
Saturated Fat:	3g	Sodium:	729mg
Cholesterol:	27mg		

Dietary Exchanges: 2 Starch, 1 Lean Meat, ½ Fat

Pasta Fazool

- 2 tablespoons olive oil
- 1 cup chopped onions
- ½ cup *each:* sliced carrots and sliced celery
- 2 cloves garlic, minced
- 4 cups chicken broth
- 1 (15-ounce) can HUNT'S® Tomato Sauce
- 1 (15-ounce) can white kidney beans, drained
- 1 (14½-ounce) can HUNT'S® Choice-Cut Diced Tomatoes with Italian Style Herbs
- 1 (8-ounce) can red kidney beans, drained
- ½ cup uncooked elbow macaroni
- 2 tablespoons chopped fresh parsley
- 2 teaspoons fresh basil leaves
- ½ teaspoon *each:* dried oregano leaves and salt
- ¼ teaspoon black pepper
- Fresh grated Parmesan cheese (optional)

In Dutch oven, heat oil and sauté onions, carrots, celery and garlic until tender. Stir in remaining ingredients except Parmesan cheese. Bring to a boil, reduce heat and simmer 10 to 15 minutes or until macaroni is tender. Sprinkle Parmesan cheese over each serving, if desired.

makes 10 servings

NUTRIENTS PER SERVING

Calories:	135	Carbohydrate:	21g
Calories from Fat:	25%	Fiber:	4g
Total Fat:	4g	Protein:	6g
Saturated Fat:	1g	Sodium:	1220mg
Cholesterol:	0mg		

Dietary Exchanges: 1 Starch, 1 Vegetable, 1 Fat

White kidney beans are often called cannellini beans. They are used in the traditional Italian version of this dish, Pasta e Fagioli, or "pasta and bean soup."

Eggplant Squash Bake

½ cup chopped onion
1 clove garlic, minced
Nonstick olive oil cooking spray
1 cup part-skim ricotta cheese
1 jar (4 ounces) diced pimiento, drained
¼ cup grated Parmesan cheese
2 tablespoons fat-free (skim) milk
1½ teaspoons dried marjoram
¾ teaspoon dried tarragon
¼ teaspoon ground nutmeg
¼ teaspoon salt
¼ teaspoon black pepper
1 cup no-sugar-added meatless spaghetti sauce, divided
½ pound eggplant, peeled and cut into thin crosswise slices
6 ounces zucchini, cut in half, then lengthwise into thin slices
6 ounces yellow summer squash, cut in half, then lengthwise into thin slices
2 tablespoons shredded part-skim mozzarella cheese

1. Combine onion and garlic in medium microwavable bowl. Spray lightly with cooking spray. Microwave at HIGH 1 minute.

2. Add next 9 ingredients, ending with pepper. Spray 9- or 10-inch round microwavable baking dish with cooking spray. Spread ⅓ cup spaghetti sauce onto bottom of dish.

3. Layer half of eggplant, zucchini and squash in dish; spoon on ricotta cheese mixture. Repeat, layering with remaining eggplant, zucchini and summer squash. Top with remaining ⅔ cup spaghetti sauce.

4. Cover with vented plastic wrap. Microwave at HIGH 17 to 19 minutes or until vegetables are tender, rotating dish every 6 minutes. Top with mozzarella cheese. Let stand 10 minutes before serving. *makes 4 servings*

NUTRIENTS PER SERVING

Calories:	190	Carbohydrate:	19g
Calories from Fat:	35%	Fiber:	5g
Total Fat:	8g	Protein:	13g
Saturated Fat:	6g	Sodium:	647mg
Cholesterol:	25mg		

Dietary Exchanges: 3 Vegetable, 1 Lean Meat, 1 Fat

Rigatoni with Fresh Tomatoes

1 cup rigatoni or mostaccioli
Nonstick cooking spray
¼ cup sliced green onions
2 cloves garlic, minced
1 cup sliced zucchini
1 teaspoon chopped fresh basil *or* ¼ teaspoon dried basil leaves, crushed
1 teaspoon chopped fresh marjoram *or* ¼ teaspoon dried marjoram leaves, crushed
⅛ teaspoon salt
⅛ teaspoon black pepper
1 cup coarsely chopped seeded Roma tomatoes
¼ cup (1 ounce) crumbled feta cheese or shredded part-skim mozzarella cheese

Prepare rigatoni according to package directions, omitting salt; drain.

Coat wok or large skillet with cooking spray; heat over medium-high heat. Add onions and garlic. Stir-fry 1 minute. Add zucchini, basil, marjoram, salt and pepper. Stir-fry 2 to 3 minutes or until zucchini is tender. Stir in tomatoes and pasta; heat through.

Divide pasta mixture onto four plates; sprinkle with cheese. *makes 4 servings*

NUTRIENTS PER SERVING

Calories:	112	Carbohydrate:	19g
Calories from Fat:	17%	Fiber:	2g
Total Fat:	2g	Protein:	5g
Saturated Fat:	1g	Sodium:	154mg
Cholesterol:	6mg		

Dietary Exchanges: 1 Starch, 1 Vegetable, ½ Fat

recipe tip

Prevent the pasta in this dish from getting too mushy by slightly undercooking it. It will continue to cook after it's mixed with the other ingredients in the wok.

Shells Florentine

- 1 cup coarsely chopped mushrooms (about 4 ounces)
- ½ cup chopped onion
- 1 clove garlic, minced
- 1 teaspoon Italian seasoning
- ¼ teaspoon ground black pepper
- 2 tablespoons FLEISCHMANN'S® Original Margarine
- 1 (16-ounce) container low-sodium, low-fat cottage cheese (1% milk fat)
- 1 (10-ounce) package frozen chopped spinach, thawed and well drained
- 6 tablespoons EGG BEATERS® Healthy Real Egg Product
- 24 jumbo macaroni shells, cooked in unsalted water and drained
- 1 (15¼-ounce) jar spaghetti sauce, divided

In large skillet, over medium-high heat, cook and stir mushrooms, onion, garlic, Italian seasoning and pepper in margarine until vegetables are tender, about 4 minutes. Remove from heat; stir in cottage cheese, spinach and Egg Beaters®. Spoon mixture into shells.

Spread ½ cup spaghetti sauce in bottom of 13×9×2-inch baking dish; arrange shells over sauce. Top with remaining sauce; cover. Bake at 350°F for 35 minutes or until hot.

makes 8 servings

microwave directions: In 1½-quart microwavable bowl, combine mushrooms, onion, garlic, Italian seasoning, black pepper and margarine; cover. Microwave at HIGH for 2 to 3 minutes or until vegetables are tender. Stir in cottage cheese, spinach and Egg Beaters®. Assemble shells as directed; spread ½ cup spaghetti sauce in bottom of 12×8×2-inch microwavable dish. Arrange shells over sauce. Top with remaining sauce; cover with plastic wrap, venting corner. Microwave at HIGH for 8 to 10 minutes or until hot. Let stand 5 minutes before serving.

Prep Time: 30 minutes
Bake Time: 35 minutes

NUTRIENTS PER SERVING

Calories:	309	Carbohydrate:	48g
Calories from Fat:	17%	Fiber:	3g
Total Fat:	6g	Protein:	16g
Saturated Fat:	1g	Sodium:	372mg
Cholesterol:	5mg		

Dietary Exchanges: 2 Starch, 2 Vegetable, 2 Lean Meat

Vegetarian Lentil Casserole

- 1 pound lentils, cooked
- ¾ cup honey
- ½ cup soy sauce
- 2 teaspoons dry mustard
- 1 teaspoon pepper
- ½ teaspoon ground ginger
- ½ cup chopped onion
- ½ cup sliced carrot
- ½ cup sliced celery
- 3 tablespoons vegetable oil
- 8 cups cooked white rice

Place lentils in 2½-quart casserole. Combine honey, soy sauce, mustard, pepper and ginger in small bowl. Gently stir into lentils. Cook and stir onion, carrot and celery in oil in small skillet over medium-high heat until onion is translucent. Add to lentils. Cover and bake at 350°F 45 minutes. Uncover and bake 15 minutes more. Serve over rice. *makes 8 servings*

Favorite recipe from **National Honey Board**

NUTRIENTS PER SERVING

Calories:	511	Carbohydrate:	99g
Calories from Fat:	10%	Fiber:	11g
Total Fat:	6g	Protein:	17g
Saturated Fat:	1g	Sodium:	1043mg
Cholesterol:	0mg		

Dietary Exchanges: 6½ Starch, 1 Fat

recipe tip

Lentils do not need to be soaked before they are cooked. Sort through them and discard any debris or blemished lentils. Then, rinse them with cold running water. Combine lentils with cold water or broth (2 cups of liquid to each 1 cup of lentils) in a saucepan. Bring to a boil. Reduce heat to low, and cover the lentils. Simmer brown and yellow varieties 15 to 20 minutes and red varieties 10 to 12 minutes or until tender.

Puerto Rican Sofrito Beans with Rice

- 1 green bell pepper, cut into quarters
- 1 small onion, cut into quarters
- ½ cup chopped fresh cilantro
- 2 tablespoons olive oil
- 1 tablespoon bottled minced garlic
- 1¼ teaspoons salt, divided
- 1 teaspoon ground cumin
- ¼ teaspoon ground red pepper
- 2 medium tomatoes, chopped
- 1 can (8 ounces) tomato sauce
- 1 can (15 ounces) black beans, rinsed and drained
- 1 can (15 ounces) red beans, rinsed and drained
- 2 cups water
- 1 cup uncooked long-grain rice

1. Place bell pepper, onion and cilantro in food processor; process until finely chopped.

2. Heat oil in large skillet over medium-high heat. Add bell pepper mixture, garlic, ½ teaspoon salt, cumin and ground red pepper; cook 5 minutes. Stir in tomatoes and tomato sauce; cook 5 minutes. Stir in beans; cook 5 minutes.

3. Combine water, rice and remaining ¾ teaspoon salt in medium saucepan. Bring to a boil over high heat. Reduce heat to low; cover and simmer 20 minutes or until water is absorbed.

4. While rice is cooking, heat bean mixture in large saucepan over low heat, stirring occasionally, until heated through (or microwave at HIGH 8 to 10 minutes, stirring after 5 minutes). Serve bean mixture with rice.

makes 8 servings

note: For a special touch, stir a handful of chopped cilantro and finely chopped red bell pepper into the rice just before serving.

serving suggestion: Press cooked rice into coffee or custard cups sprayed with nonstick cooking spray. Unmold onto individual plates or bowls; serve bean mixture around rice.

NUTRIENTS PER SERVING

Calories:	229	Carbohydrate:	41g
Calories from Fat:	22%	Fiber:	8g
Total Fat:	6g	Protein:	8g
Saturated Fat:	1g	Sodium:	1058mg
Cholesterol:	0mg		

Dietary Exchanges: 2½ Starch, 3 Vegetable, 1 Fat

Cheesy Enchiladas

- 1 package (8 ounces) PHILADELPHIA FREE® Fat Free Cream Cheese, softened
- 1 package (8 ounces) KRAFT FREE® Fat Free Natural Shredded Non-Fat Cheddar Cheese, divided
- ¼ cup sliced green onions
- 6 flour tortillas (6 inch)
- 1 cup TACO BELL® HOME ORIGINALS™* Thick 'N Chunky Salsa

**TACO BELL and HOME ORIGINALS are registered trademarks owned and licensed by Taco Bell Corp.*

BEAT cream cheese with electric mixer on medium speed until smooth. Add 1 cup of the cheddar cheese and onions, mixing until blended.

SPREAD ¼ cup cream cheese mixture down center of each tortilla; roll up. Place, seam side down, in 11×7-inch baking dish. Pour salsa over tortillas. Sprinkle with remaining cheddar cheese; cover.

BAKE at 350°F for 20 to 25 minutes or until thoroughly heated.

makes 6 servings

Prep: 15 minutes
Bake: 25 minutes

NUTRIENTS PER SERVING

1 enchilada = 1 serving

Calories:	228	Carbohydrate:	28g
Calories from Fat:	13%	Fiber:	4g
Total Fat:	3g	Protein:	21g
Saturated Fat:	1g	Sodium:	940mg
Cholesterol:	3mg		

Dietary Exchanges: 2 Starch, 2 Lean Meat

Cheesy Enchilada

Healthy Fettuccine Primavera

- 1 can (10¾ ounces) reduced-fat condensed cream of chicken soup
- ⅓ cup fat-free (skim) milk
- 2 cloves garlic, minced
- ½ teaspoon salt
- ½ teaspoon dried Italian seasoning
- ⅛ teaspoon fennel seeds, crushed
- Nonstick cooking spray
- 4 cups sliced fresh vegetables (peppers, zucchini, carrots, asparagus) or thawed frozen vegetables
- 1 cup coarsely chopped fresh plum tomatoes
- 4 cups hot cooked fettuccine

Combine soup, milk, garlic, salt, Italian seasoning and fennel in small bowl; set aside. Spray large nonstick skillet with cooking spray. Sauté vegetables over medium heat 4 to 5 minutes. Stir in soup mixture; simmer 3 to 4 minutes. Add tomato; mix well. Serve over hot fettuccine.

makes 6 servings

NUTRIENTS PER SERVING

Calories:	178	Carbohydrate:	34g
Calories from Fat:	13%	Fiber:	4g
Total Fat:	3g	Protein:	7g
Saturated Fat:	1g	Sodium:	616mg
Cholesterol:	7mg		

Dietary Exchanges: 2 Starch, 1 Vegetable, ½ Fat

Tip

Primavera is an Italian word meaning "springtime." You will most often see it used in the titles of recipes that include fresh spring vegetables—either raw or blanched.

Today's Slim Ricotta Spinach Rolls

SAUCE

1 medium onion, finely chopped
2 cloves garlic, minced
1 tablespoon butter
3 cups no-salt-added tomato sauce
1 teaspoon dried oregano leaves
½ teaspoon dried thyme leaves
½ teaspoon dried basil leaves
¼ teaspoon dried marjoram leaves

FILLING

1 package (10 ounces) frozen chopped spinach
1 cup (8 ounces) Wisconsin part-skim ricotta cheese
2 tablespoons Wisconsin Parmesan cheese
⅛ teaspoon ground nutmeg
Dash ground black pepper
8 lasagna noodles, cooked and drained

Cook and stir onion and garlic in butter in large skillet over medium heat until tender. Add tomato sauce and seasonings. Reduce heat; simmer 30 minutes, stirring occasionally. Prepare spinach according to package directions. Drain and squeeze out excess water. In medium bowl, combine spinach, cheeses, nutmeg and pepper until thoroughly mixed.

Preheat oven to 350°F. Spread spinach mixture evenly along entire length of each noodle. Roll up each noodle lengthwise and place on its side in a buttered shallow baking dish. Pour sauce over rolls. Bake 20 to 30 minutes or until heated through. *makes 4 servings*

Favorite recipe from **Wisconsin Milk Marketing Board**

NUTRIENTS PER SERVING

2 rolls = 1 serving

Calories:	417	Carbohydrate:	62g
Calories from Fat:	22%	Fiber:	8g
Total Fat:	11g	Protein:	21g
Saturated Fat:	5g	Sodium:	253mg
Cholesterol:	29mg		

Dietary Exchanges: 4 Starch, 1 Lean Meat 1½ Fat

Lentil and Brown Rice Soup

- 1 envelope LIPTON® RECIPE SECRETS® Onion Recipe Soup Mix*
- 4 cups water
- ¾ cup lentils, rinsed and drained
- ½ cup uncooked brown or regular rice
- 1 can (14½ ounces) whole peeled tomatoes, undrained, coarsely chopped
- 1 medium carrot, coarsely chopped
- 1 large stalk celery, coarsely chopped
- ½ teaspoon dried basil leaves
- ½ teaspoon dried oregano leaves
- ¼ teaspoon dried thyme leaves (optional)
- 1 tablespoon finely chopped fresh parsley
- 1 tablespoon apple cider vinegar
- ¼ teaspoon pepper

**Also terrific with LIPTON® Recipe Secrets Beefy Onion or Beefy Mushroom Recipe Soup Mix.*

In large saucepan or stockpot, combine onion recipe soup mix, water, lentils, uncooked rice, tomatoes with liquid, carrot, celery, basil, oregano and thyme. Bring to a boil, then simmer covered, stirring occasionally, 45 minutes or until lentils and rice are tender. Stir in remaining ingredients. *makes about 3 servings*

NUTRIENTS PER SERVING

2 cups = 1 serving

Calories:	345	Carbohydrate:	66g
Calories from Fat:	4%	Fiber:	18g
Total Fat:	2g	Protein:	19g
Saturated Fat:	<1g	Sodium:	1043mg
Cholesterol:	0mg		

Dietary Exchanges: 4 Starch, 1 Vegetable

recipe tip

This soup is packed with fiber. Foods with fiber may fill you up and help you eat less. Plus, the National Cancer Institute recommends getting between 25 to 35 grams of fiber a day. By eating this soup, you'll be well on your way to meeting that goal.

Veggie Tostadas

1 tablespoon olive oil
1 cup chopped onion
1 cup chopped celery
2 large cloves garlic, chopped
1 can (15½ ounces) red kidney beans, drained
1 can (15½ ounces) Great Northern beans, drained
1 can (14½ ounces) salsa-style diced tomatoes
2 teaspoons mild chili powder
1 teaspoon cumin
2 tablespoons chopped fresh cilantro
6 small corn tortillas
Toppings: shredded lettuce, chopped tomatoes, shredded Cheddar cheese and sour cream

Heat oil in large skillet over medium heat. Add onion, celery and garlic. Cook and stir 8 minutes or until softened. Add beans and tomatoes. Stir to blend. Add chili powder and cumin; stir. Reduce heat to medium-low. Simmer 30 minutes, stirring occasionally, until thickened.

Preheat oven to 400°F.

While bean mixture simmers, place tortillas in single layer directly on oven rack. Bake 10 to 12 minutes or until crisp. Place one tortilla on each plate. Spoon bean mixture evenly over each one. Top with lettuce, tomatoes, Cheddar cheese and sour cream to taste. *makes 6 servings*

NUTRIENTS PER SERVING

1 tostada = 1 serving

Calories:	208	Carbohydrate:	39g
Calories from Fat:	13%	Fiber:	10g
Total Fat:	3g	Protein:	10g
Saturated Fat:	<1g	Sodium:	945mg
Cholesterol:	0mg		

Dietary Exchanges: 2 Starch, 2 Vegetable, ½ Fat

Veggie Tostada

Salad for Supper

Zesty Romaine and Pasta Salad

- 6 ounces bowtie pasta
- 1 cup broccoli florets
- ¼ cup red wine vinegar
- ¼ cup water
- 2 tablespoons sugar
- 1 tablespoon finely chopped fresh basil
- 1 tablespoon lemon juice
- 1 tablespoon prepared Dijon mustard
- 1 clove garlic, minced
- ½ teaspoon black pepper
- 6 cups washed and chopped romaine lettuce
- 1 can (15 ounces) dark red kidney beans, drained and rinsed
- 1 cup carrot slices
- 1 small red onion, cut into halves and thinly sliced
- ½ cup grated Parmesan cheese

1. Cook pasta according to package directions, adding broccoli during last 3 minutes of cooking; drain. Rinse with cold water; drain.

2. To make dressing, combine vinegar, ¼ cup water, sugar, basil, lemon juice, mustard, garlic and pepper in small bowl until well blended.

3. Combine lettuce, pasta, broccoli, beans, carrots and onion in large bowl. Add dressing; toss to coat. Sprinkle with Parmesan cheese.

makes 4 servings

NUTRIENTS PER SERVING

Calories:	276	Carbohydrate:	58g
Calories from Fat:	5%	Fiber:	12g
Total Fat:	2g	Protein:	15g
Saturated Fat:	<1g	Sodium:	230mg
Cholesterol:	0mg		

Dietary Exchanges: 3 Starch, 2 Vegetable, ½ Lean Meat

Grilled Steak and Asparagus Salad

- ½ cup bottled light olive oil vinaigrette dressing
- ⅓ cup A.1.® Steak Sauce
- 1 (1-pound) beef top round steak
- 1 (10-ounce) package frozen asparagus spears, cooked and cooled
- ½ cup thinly sliced red bell pepper
- 8 large lettuce leaves
- 1 tablespoon toasted sesame seeds

Blend vinaigrette and steak sauce. Pour marinade over steak in nonmetal dish. Cover; refrigerate 1 hour.

Remove steak from marinade; reserve marinade. Grill or broil steak 4 inches from heat source 5 minutes, basting occasionally with marinade. Turn steak and baste with marinade once more. Grill or broil 5 minutes more or until desired doneness.

Thinly slice steak; arrange steak, asparagus and red pepper on lettuce leaves. Heat marinade to a boil; pour over salad. Sprinkle with sesame seeds; serve immediately.

makes 4 servings

NUTRIENTS PER SERVING

Calories:	230	Carbohydrate:	15g
Calories from Fat:	24%	Fiber:	2g
Total Fat:	6g	Protein:	29g
Saturated Fat:	2g	Sodium:	468mg
Cholesterol:	56mg		

Dietary Exchanges: 2 Vegetable, 3 Lean Meat

Crab Cobb Salad

- 12 cups washed and torn romaine lettuce
- 2 cans (6 ounces each) crabmeat, drained
- 2 cups diced ripe tomatoes or halved cherry tomatoes
- ¼ cup (1½ ounces) crumbled blue or Gorgonzola cheese
- ¼ cup cholesterol-free bacon bits
- ¾ cup fat-free Italian or Caesar salad dressing
- Black pepper

Arrange lettuce on large serving platter. Arrange crabmeat, tomatoes, blue cheese and bacon bits in rows attractively over lettuce. Just before serving, drizzle dressing evenly over salad; toss. Sprinkle with pepper to taste.

makes 8 servings

NUTRIENTS PER SERVING

Calories:	110	Carbohydrate:	8g
Calories from Fat:	27%	Fiber:	2g
Total Fat:	3g	Protein:	12g
Saturated Fat:	1g	Sodium:	666mg
Cholesterol:	46mg		

Dietary Exchanges: 1½ Vegetable, 1½ Lean Meat

Cool and Creamy Pea Salad with Cucumbers and Red Onion

- 2 tablespoons finely chopped red onion
- 1 tablespoon reduced-fat mayonnaise
- ⅛ teaspoon salt
- ⅛ teaspoon black pepper
- ½ cup frozen green peas, thawed
- ¼ cup diced red bell pepper
- ¼ cup diced cucumber

Combine onion, mayonnaise, salt and pepper in medium bowl; stir until well blended. Add remaining ingredients; toss gently to coat.

makes 2 servings

NUTRIENTS PER SERVING

½ cup = 1 serving

Calories:	65	Carbohydrate:	8g
Calories from Fat:	36%	Fiber:	3g
Total Fat:	3g	Protein:	2g
Saturated Fat:	1g	Sodium:	238mg
Cholesterol:	3mg		

Dietary Exchanges: 1 Vegetable, ½ Fat

Crab Cobb Salad

Chicken and Spinach Salad

12 ounces chicken tenders
Nonstick cooking spray
4 cups shredded spinach
2 cups washed and torn romaine lettuce
8 thin slices red onion
2 tablespoons (½ ounce) crumbled blue cheese
1 large grapefruit, peeled and sectioned
½ cup frozen citrus blend concentrate, thawed
¼ cup prepared fat-free Italian salad dressing

1. Cut chicken into 2×½-inch strips. Spray large nonstick skillet with cooking spray; heat over medium heat until hot. Add chicken; cook and stir 5 minutes or until no longer pink in center. Remove from skillet.

2. Divide spinach, lettuce, onion, cheese, grapefruit and chicken among 4 salad plates. Combine citrus blend concentrate and Italian dressing in small bowl; drizzle over salads. Garnish with assorted greens, if desired.

makes 4 servings

NUTRIENTS PER SERVING

Calories:	218	Carbohydrate:	23g
Calories from Fat:	15%	Fiber:	3g
Total Fat:	4g	Protein:	23g
Saturated Fat:	1g	Sodium:	361mg
Cholesterol:	55mg		

Dietary Exchanges: 1½ Fruit, 1 Vegetable, 2 Lean Meat

Tip

Chicken "tenders," or "supremes," are the lean, tender strips found on the underside of the breast. They are skinless and boneless and have virtually no waste.

Low Fat Watergate Salad

1 package (4-serving size) JELL-O® Pistachio Flavor Fat Free Sugar Free Instant Reduced Calorie Pudding & Pie Filling
1 can (8 ounces) crushed pineapple in juice, undrained
1 container (8 ounces) BREYERS®* Vanilla Lowfat Yogurt
2 cups plus 6 tablespoons thawed COOL WHIP FREE® Whipped Topping, divided

**BREYERS® is a registered trademark of Unilever, N.V., used under license.*

STIR pudding mix, pineapple with juice and yogurt in large bowl until well blended. Gently stir in 2 cups of the whipped topping.

REFRIGERATE 1 hour or until ready to serve. Top each serving with 1 tablespoon remaining whipped topping.

makes 6 servings

Prep: 10 minutes plus refrigerating

NUTRIENTS PER SERVING

Calories:	130	Carbohydrate:	26g
Calories from Fat:	14%	Fiber:	0g
Total Fat:	2g	Protein:	2g
Saturated Fat:	2g	Sodium:	220mg
Cholesterol:	<1mg		

Dietary Exchanges: 1½ Starch

recipe tip

An 8-ounce tub of COOL WHIP Lite/Free® holds about 3¼ cups of whipped topping. Thawing is easy. Just place the unopened frozen 8-ounce tub in the refrigerator for 4 hours. Don't try to thaw whipped topping in the microwave.

White and Black Bean Salad

- 1 cup finely chopped red onions
- 2 cloves garlic, minced
- 2 tablespoons olive oil or vegetable oil
- ⅓ cup red wine vinegar
- ¼ cup chopped red bell pepper
- ¼ cup chopped green bell pepper
- 2 tablespoons minced parsley
- 1 teaspoon EQUAL® FOR RECIPES *or* 3 packets EQUAL® sweetener *or* 2 tablespoons EQUAL® SPOONFUL™
- ¼ teaspoon salt
- ¼ teaspoon pepper
- 1 can (15 ounces) great Northern beans, rinsed and drained
- 1 can (15 ounces) black beans, rinsed and drained
- Red and green bell pepper rings

• Sauté onions and garlic in oil until crisp-tender in medium skillet; remove from heat and cool until warm. Stir in vinegar, chopped peppers, parsley, Equal®, salt and pepper.

• Pour onion mixture over combined beans in serving bowl; mix well. Garnish with pepper rings.

makes 8 servings

NUTRIENTS PER SERVING

Calories:	103	Carbohydrate:	17g
Calories from Fat:	25%	Fiber:	6g
Total Fat:	3g	Protein:	5g
Saturated Fat:	<1g	Sodium:	497mg
Cholesterol:	0mg		

Dietary Exchanges: 1 Starch, ½ Fat

High in fiber and low in fat, this vegetarian salad is one healthy dinner idea. Team it with a whole-wheat roll, and you've got a complete meal!

Jerk Turkey Salad

- 6 ounces turkey breast tenderloin
- 1 tablespoon Caribbean jerk seasoning
- 4 cups packaged mixed salad greens
- ¾ cup sliced peeled cucumber
- ⅔ cup chopped fresh pineapple
- ⅔ cup quartered strawberries or raspberries
- ½ cup slivered peeled jicama or sliced celery
- 1 green onion, sliced
- ¼ cup lime juice
- 3 tablespoons honey

1. Prepare grill for direct grilling. Rub turkey with jerk seasoning.

2. Grill turkey over medium coals 15 to 20 minutes or until turkey is no longer pink and juices run clear, turning once. Remove from grill and cool.

3. Cut turkey into bite-size pieces. Toss together greens, turkey, cucumber, pineapple, strawberries, jicama and green onion.

4. Combine lime juice and honey. Toss with greens mixture. Serve immediately. *makes 2 servings*

NUTRIENTS PER SERVING

Calories:	265	Carbohydrate:	48g
Calories from Fat:	6%	Fiber:	6g
Total Fat:	2g	Protein:	17g
Saturated Fat:	1g	Sodium:	356mg
Cholesterol:	34mg		

Dietary Exchanges: 2 Fruit, 2 Vegetable, 2 Lean Meat

Jamaican Seafood Salad

- 6 ounces uncooked vermicelli noodles
- 6 ounces fresh or imitation crabmeat
- 4 ounces cooked medium shrimp
- 1 cup diagonally sliced yellow squash
- 1 cup diagonally sliced zucchini
- 1 tablespoon rice wine vinegar
- 1 tablespoon reduced-sodium soy sauce
- 1 tablespoon minced fresh cilantro
- 1 tablespoon lime juice
- 2 teaspoons dark sesame oil
- 2 teaspoons grated fresh ginger
- 1 teaspoon grated lime peel
- ⅛ teaspoon ground cinnamon

1. Cook noodles according to package directions, omitting salt. Drain and rinse well under cold water until pasta is cool; drain well.

2. Combine crabmeat, shrimp, yellow squash and zucchini in medium bowl.

3. Combine vinegar, soy sauce, cilantro, lime juice, sesame oil, ginger, lime peel and cinnamon in small bowl; pour over vegetable mixture.

4. Toss to coat evenly. Serve over noodles, chilled or at room temperature. *makes 6 servings*

NUTRIENTS PER SERVING

1 cup = 1 serving

Calories:	176	Carbohydrate:	23g
Calories from Fat:	14%	Fiber:	2g
Total Fat:	3g	Protein:	14g
Saturated Fat:	<1g	Sodium:	439mg
Cholesterol:	52mg		

Dietary Exchanges: 1 Starch, 1 Vegetable, 1 Lean Meat

Zesty Pasta Salad

- 3 ounces uncooked tri-color rotini pasta
- 1 cup sliced mushrooms
- ¾ cup pasta-ready canned tomatoes, undrained
- ½ cup sliced green bell pepper
- ¼ cup chopped onion
- ¼ cup fat-free Italian salad dressing
- 2 tablespoons grated Parmesan cheese
- Lettuce leaves for garnish (optional)

1. Cook pasta according to package directions, omitting salt. Rinse with cool water; drain. Cool.

2. Combine pasta, mushrooms, tomatoes with liquid, pepper and onion in large bowl. Pour Italian dressing over pasta mixture; toss to coat.

3. Top with cheese before serving. Garnish with lettuce leaves, if desired. *makes 6 servings*

NUTRIENTS PER SERVING

Calories:	80	Carbohydrate:	13g
Calories from Fat:	19%	Fiber:	1g
Total Fat:	2g	Protein:	4g
Saturated Fat:	<1g	Sodium:	239mg
Cholesterol:	2mg		

Dietary Exchanges: ½ Starch, 1 Vegetable

recipe tip

This salad can either be served immediately, or chilled and served later as a cold salad.

Strawberry Banana Salad

1½ cups boiling water
1 package (8-serving size) or 2 packages (4-serving size each) JELL-O® Brand Strawberry or Strawberry Banana Flavor Sugar Free Low Calorie Gelatin
2 cups cold water
1 cup chopped strawberries
1 banana, sliced

STIR boiling water into gelatin in large bowl at least 2 minutes until completely dissolved. Stir in cold water. Refrigerate about 1½ hours or until thickened (spoon drawn through leaves definite impression).

STIR in strawberries and banana. Pour into 5-cup mold that has been sprayed with no stick cooking spray.

REFRIGERATE 4 hours or until firm. Unmold. Store leftover gelatin mold in refrigerator. *makes 10 servings*

Prep Time: 15 minutes
Refrigerate Time: 5½ hours

NUTRIENTS PER SERVING

½ cup = 1 serving

Calories:	22	Carbohydrate:	4g
Calories from Fat:	4%	Fiber:	1g
Total Fat:	<1g	Protein:	1g
Saturated Fat:	<1g	Sodium:	43mg
Cholesterol:	0mg		

Dietary Exchanges: ½ Fruit

Mixed Greens with Honey Raspberry Vinaigrette

- ¼ cup raspberry vinegar or balsamic vinegar
- ¼ cup honey
- 1 tablespoon olive oil
- ½ teaspoon chopped fresh oregano, basil or thyme
- 8 cups mixed lettuce greens

Combine vinegar and honey in small bowl; mix well. To serve, drizzle 2 to 3 tablespoons vinegar-honey mixture, oil and oregano over lettuce greens. Toss to coat. Garnish with fruit, if desired. *makes 4 servings*

variation: Use 2 to 3 tablespoons chopped fresh mint for mixed fruit salads in place of oregano, basil or thyme.

note: Vinegar-honey mixture may be stored in covered jar for future use.

Favorite recipe from **National Honey Board**

NUTRIENTS PER SERVING

Calories:	111	Carbohydrate:	21g
Calories from Fat:	27%	Fiber:	2g
Total Fat:	4g	Protein:	2g
Saturated Fat:	<1g	Sodium:	10mg
Cholesterol:	0mg		

Dietary Exchanges: 1 Fruit, 1 Vegetable, ½ Fat

Gazpacho Salad

1½ cups peeled and coarsely chopped tomatoes*
1 cup peeled, seeded and diced cucumber
¾ cup chopped onion
½ cup chopped red bell pepper
½ cup fresh or frozen corn kernels, cooked and drained
1 tablespoon lime juice
1 tablespoon red wine vinegar
2 teaspoons water
1 teaspoon extra-virgin olive oil
1 teaspoon minced fresh garlic
¼ teaspoon salt
¼ teaspoon black pepper
Pinch ground red pepper
1 medium head romaine lettuce, torn into bite-size pieces
1 cup peeled and diced jicama
½ cup fresh cilantro

**To peel tomatoes easily, blanch in boiling water 30 seconds; immediately transfer to bowl of cold water, then peel.*

1. Combine tomatoes, cucumber, onion, bell pepper and corn in large bowl. Combine lime juice, vinegar, water, oil, garlic, salt, black pepper and ground red pepper in small bowl; whisk until well blended. Pour over tomato mixture; toss well. Cover and refrigerate several hours to allow flavors to blend.

2. Toss together lettuce, jicama and cilantro in another large bowl. Divide lettuce mixture evenly among 6 plates. Place ⅔ cup chilled tomato mixture on top of lettuce, spreading to edges.

makes 6 servings

NUTRIENTS PER SERVING

Calories:	71	Carbohydrate:	14g
Calories from Fat:	14%	Fiber:	3g
Total Fat:	1g	Protein:	3g
Saturated Fat:	<1g	Sodium:	105mg
Cholesterol:	0mg		

Dietary Exchanges: 3 Vegetable

Smoked Turkey Pasta Salad

8 ounces uncooked ditalini pasta (small tubes)
6 ounces smoked turkey or chicken breast, skin removed, cut into strips
1 can (15 ounces) light kidney beans, rinsed and drained
½ cup thinly sliced celery
¼ cup chopped red onion
⅓ cup reduced-fat mayonnaise
2 tablespoons balsamic vinegar
2 tablespoons snipped fresh chives or green onion
1 tablespoon fresh tarragon *or* 1½ teaspoons dried tarragon leaves
1 teaspoon Dijon mustard
1 clove garlic, minced
¼ teaspoon black pepper
Lettuce leaves (optional)

1. Cook pasta according to package directions, omitting salt. Drain and rinse well under cold water until pasta is cool; drain well.

2. Combine pasta with turkey, beans, celery and onion in medium bowl. Combine mayonnaise, vinegar, chives, tarragon, mustard, garlic and pepper in small bowl. Pour over pasta mixture; toss to coat evenly. Serve on lettuce leaves, if desired. *makes 7 servings*

NUTRIENTS PER SERVING

1 cup = 1 serving

Calories:	233	Carbohydrate:	34g
Calories from Fat:	19%	Fiber:	5g
Total Fat:	5g	Protein:	13g
Saturated Fat:	1g	Sodium:	249mg
Cholesterol:	12mg		

Dietary Exchanges: 2 Starch, 1 Lean Meat, ½ Fat

Sensational Spinach Salad with Orange Poppy Seed Vinaigrette

- ¼ cup orange juice
- 3 tablespoons red wine vinegar
- 2 tablespoons sugar
- 1 tablespoon olive oil
- 1 teaspoon grated orange peel
- 1 teaspoon poppy seeds
- ¼ teaspoon salt
- 9 cups washed and torn spinach leaves
- 1 can (15 ounces) chilled mandarin orange segments, drained
- 1½ cups fresh sliced mushrooms
- 1 small red onion, sliced and separated into rings
- 3 cooked egg whites, coarsely chopped

1. To prepare vinaigrette, combine orange juice, red wine vinegar, sugar, oil, orange peel, poppy seeds and salt in small bowl until well blended.

2. To prepare salad, combine spinach, orange segments, mushrooms, onion and egg whites in large serving bowl. Pour vinaigrette over spinach mixture just before serving; toss to coat. Serve immediately. *makes 6 servings*

NUTRIENTS PER SERVING

Calories:	106	Carbohydrate:	17g
Calories from Fat:	22%	Fiber:	3g
Total Fat:	3g	Protein:	5g
Saturated Fat:	<1g	Sodium:	196mg
Cholesterol:	0mg		

Dietary Exchanges: 3 Vegetable, ½ Fat

recipe tip

One pound of fresh spinach yields about 10 to 12 cups of torn pieces.

Chicken Waldorf Salad

2 cups cubed or shredded cooked chicken breast
2 cups chopped, cored Red Delicious apples
1 cup sliced celery
⅔ cup halved seedless grapes
¼ cup chopped pecans, toasted
½ cup fat-free mayonnaise
½ cup fat-free sour cream
3 to 4 teaspoons lemon juice
2 teaspoons Dijon-style mustard
2½ teaspoons EQUAL® FOR RECIPES *or* 8 packets EQUAL® sweetener *or* ⅓ cup EQUAL® SPOONFUL™
Salt and pepper
Red leaf lettuce
¼ cup chopped pecans (optional)

• Combine chicken, apples, celery, grapes and ¼ cup pecans in bowl. Blend mayonnaise, sour cream, lemon juice, mustard and Equal®; stir into chicken mixture. Season to taste with salt and pepper.

• Spoon salad onto lettuce-lined plates; sprinkle with ¼ cup pecans, if desired. *makes 4 servings*

NUTRIENTS PER SERVING

Calories:	308	Carbohydrate:	30g
Calories from Fat:	26%	Fiber:	3g
Total Fat:	9g	Protein:	27g
Saturated Fat:	1g	Sodium:	330mg
Cholesterol:	60mg		

Dietary Exchanges: 2 Fruit, 3 Lean Meat

Beef Salad

DRESSING:

1 (6-ounce) container plain non-fat yogurt
1 tablespoon water
2 teaspoons minced fresh onion
1 teaspoon minced fresh garlic
½ teaspoon salt
¼ teaspoon celery seed
¼ teaspoon pepper

SALAD:

WESSON® No-Stick Cooking Spray
1 (6-ounce) package frozen pea pods, thawed and drained
1 cup onion, sliced into rings
12 ounces cooked lean beef, cut in julienne strips
1 tomato, cut in thin wedges
1 head butter lettuce, washed and drained

DRESSING

In small bowl, combine *all* dressing ingredients; mix well. Set aside.

SALAD

1. Spray skillet with WESSON® Cooking Spray. Sauté pea pods and onion until tender. Remove from heat.

2. In bowl, combine pea pod mixture, beef and tomatoes; chill.

3. Serve on bed of lettuce with savory dressing.

makes 4 (13-ounce) servings

serving suggestion: You may substitute any lean meat, poultry or fish.

NUTRIENTS PER SERVING

13 ounces salad = 1 serving

Calories:	250	Carbohydrate:	13g
Calories from Fat:	29%	Fiber:	3g
Total Fat:	8g	Protein:	31g
Saturated Fat:	3g	Sodium:	389mg
Cholesterol:	74mg		

Dietary Exchanges: 3 Vegetable, 3 Lean Meat

Rainbow Fruit Salad with Yogurt Sauce

1 medium pear, sliced
1 medium navel orange, peeled and cut into segments
1 cup sliced strawberries
¾ cup seedless red grapes
1 kiwifruit, peeled and chopped
2 tablespoons lemon juice
1 container (8 ounces) plain nonfat yogurt
2 tablespoons packed brown sugar
¼ teaspoon ground cinnamon
1 medium cantaloupe

1. Combine pear, orange, strawberries, grapes and kiwi in large bowl. Pour lemon juice over fruit; toss gently to coat.

2. Blend yogurt, brown sugar and cinnamon in small bowl until smooth.

3. Cut cantaloupe in half between stem and blossom ends. Scoop out and discard seeds. Carefully slice cantaloupe into 4 rings about 1 inch thick.

4. Place cantaloupe rings on each of 4 plates. Fill center of each ring with fruit salad; drizzle with yogurt mixture.

makes 4 servings

Prep Time: 15 minutes

NUTRIENTS PER SERVING

Calories:	231	Carbohydrate:	55g
Calories from Fat:	3%	Fiber:	7g
Total Fat:	1g	Protein:	7g
Saturated Fat:	<1g	Sodium:	110mg
Cholesterol:	1mg		

Dietary Exchanges: ½ Milk, 3 Fruit

Santa Fe Grilled Vegetable Salad

2 baby eggplants (6 ounces each), halved
1 medium yellow summer squash, halved
1 medium zucchini, halved
1 green bell pepper, cored and quartered
1 red bell pepper, cored and quartered
1 small onion, peeled and halved
½ cup orange juice
2 tablespoons lime juice
1 tablespoon olive oil
2 cloves garlic, minced
1 teaspoon dried oregano leaves
¼ teaspoon salt
¼ teaspoon ground red pepper
¼ teaspoon black pepper
2 tablespoons chopped fresh cilantro

1. Combine all ingredients except cilantro in large bowl; toss to coat.

2. To prevent sticking, spray grid with nonstick cooking spray. Prepare coals for direct grilling. Place vegetables on grill, 2 to 3 inches from hot coals; reserve marinade. Grill 3 to 4 minutes per side or until tender and lightly charred; cool 10 minutes. Or, place vegetables on rack of broiler pan coated with nonstick cooking spray; reserve marinade. Broil 2 to 3 inches from heat, 3 to 4 minutes per side or until tender; cool 10 minutes.

3. Remove peel from eggplant, if desired. Slice vegetables into bite-size pieces; return to marinade. Stir in cilantro; toss to coat.

makes 8 servings

NUTRIENTS PER SERVING

Calories:	63	Carbohydrate:	11g
Calories from Fat:	27%	Fiber:	1g
Total Fat:	2g	Protein:	2g
Saturated Fat:	<1g	Sodium:	70mg
Cholesterol:	<1mg		

Dietary Exchanges: 2 Vegetable, ½ Fat

Broiled Tuna and Raspberry Salad

- ½ cup fat-free ranch salad dressing
- ¼ cup raspberry vinegar
- 1½ teaspoons Cajun seasoning
- 1 thick-sliced tuna steak (about 6 to 8 ounces)
- 2 cups torn romaine lettuce leaves
- 1 cup torn mixed baby lettuce leaves
- ½ cup fresh raspberries

1. Combine salad dressing, vinegar and Cajun seasoning. Pour ¼ cup salad dressing mixture into resealable plastic food storage bag to use as marinade, reserving remaining mixture. Add tuna to marinade. Seal bag; turn to coat. Marinate in refrigerator 10 minutes, turning once.

2. Preheat broiler. Spray rack of broiler pan with nonstick cooking spray. Place tuna on rack. Broil tuna 4 inches from heat 5 minutes. Turn tuna and brush with marinade; discard remaining marinade. Broil 5 minutes more or until tuna flakes in center. Cool 5 minutes. Cut into ¼-inch slices.

3. Toss lettuces together in large bowl; divide evenly between two serving plates. Top with tuna and raspberries; drizzle with reserved salad dressing mixture.

makes 2 servings

Prep and Cook Time: 27 minutes

NUTRIENTS PER SERVING

Calories:	215	Carbohydrate:	18g
Calories from Fat:	22%	Fiber:	5g
Total Fat:	5g	Protein:	24g
Saturated Fat:	1g	Sodium:	427mg
Cholesterol:	35mg		

Dietary Exchanges: ½ Fruit, 1 Vegetable, 3 Lean Meat

Turkey, Mandarin and Poppy Seed Salad

- ¼ cup orange juice
- 1½ tablespoons red wine vinegar
- 1½ teaspoons poppy seeds
- 1½ teaspoons olive oil
- 1 teaspoon Dijon-style mustard
- ⅛ teaspoon ground pepper
- 5 cups torn stemmed washed red leaf lettuce
- 2 cups torn stemmed washed spinach
- ½ pound honey roasted turkey breast, cut into ½-inch julienne strips
- 1 can (10½ ounces) mandarin oranges, drained

In small bowl, combine orange juice, vinegar, poppy seeds, oil, mustard and pepper. Set aside. In large bowl, toss together lettuce, spinach, turkey and oranges. Pour dressing over turkey mixture and serve immediately.

makes 4 servings

Favorite recipe from **National Turkey Federation**

NUTRIENTS PER SERVING

Calories:	136	Carbohydrate:	15g
Calories from Fat:	23%	Fiber:	2g
Total Fat:	4g	Protein:	13g
Saturated Fat:	<1g	Sodium:	688mg
Cholesterol:	20mg		

Dietary Exchanges: ½ Fruit, 1 Vegetable, 2 Lean Meat

recipe tip

To julienne a food, cut it into thin, four-sided strips.

Saucy Potato Salad

¼ cup chopped onion
1 (16-ounce) jar MOTT'S® Apple Sauce
⅓ cup vinegar
¼ cup thinly sliced celery
1 tablespoon Dijon-style mustard *or* ½ teaspoon dry mustard
8 medium red-skinned potatoes (about 3 pounds), peeled, cooked and sliced
¾ cup chopped dill pickle
Salt (optional)
Pepper (optional)

1. Spray large nonstick saucepan with nonstick cooking spray; heat over medium heat until hot. Add onion; cook and stir about 3 minutes or until transparent.

2. Stir in apple sauce, vinegar, celery and mustard. Increase heat to high; bring mixture to a boil, stirring occasionally.

3. Place potatoes in large bowl; add pickle. Pour hot apple sauce mixture over potato mixture; toss until well coated. Add salt and pepper, if desired. Serve immediately or cover and refrigerate until serving. Refrigerate leftovers.

makes 8 servings

NUTRIENTS PER SERVING

Calories:	147	Carbohydrate:	38g
Calories from Fat:	1%	Fiber:	3g
Total Fat:	<1g	Protein:	2g
Saturated Fat:	<1g	Sodium:	263mg
Cholesterol:	<1mg		

Dietary Exchanges: 2 Starch

Fajita Salad

- 1 beef sirloin steak (6 ounces)
- ¼ cup fresh lime juice
- 2 tablespoons chopped fresh cilantro
- 1 clove garlic, minced
- 1 teaspoon chili powder
- 2 red bell peppers
- 1 medium onion
- 1 teaspoon olive oil
- 1 cup garbanzo beans, rinsed and drained
- 4 cups mixed salad greens
- 1 tomato, cut into wedges
- 1 cup salsa
- Sour cream (optional)
- Cilantro sprigs (optional)

1. Cut beef into 2×1×¼-inch strips. Place in resealable plastic food storage bag. Combine lime juice, cilantro, garlic and chili powder in small bowl. Pour over beef; seal bag. Let stand for 10 minutes, turning once.

2. Cut bell peppers into strips. Cut onion into slices. Heat olive oil in large nonstick skillet over medium-high heat until hot. Add bell peppers and onion. Cook and stir 6 minutes or until vegetables are crisp-tender. Remove from skillet. Add beef and marinade to skillet. Cook and stir 3 minutes or until meat is cooked through. Remove from heat. Add bell peppers, onion and garbanzo beans to skillet; toss to coat with pan juices. Cool slightly.

3. Divide salad greens evenly among serving plates. Top with beef mixture and tomato wedges. Serve with salsa. Garnish with sour cream and sprigs of cilantro, if desired.

makes 4 servings

NUTRIENTS PER SERVING

Calories:	181	Carbohydrate:	25g
Calories from Fat:	18%	Fiber:	6g
Total Fat:	4g	Protein:	16g
Saturated Fat:	1g	Sodium:	698mg
Cholesterol:	22mg		

Dietary Exchanges: 1½ Starch, 1½ Lean Meat

Mediterranean Chicken Salad

- 1 box (5¼ ounces) quick-cooking bulgur wheat
- ¾ pound chicken tenders
- 1 tablespoon olive oil
- 1 cup chopped tomato
- 1 cup chopped fresh parsley
- 2 green onions, sliced
- 2 tablespoons lemon juice
- Salt (optional)
- Black pepper

1. Prepare bulgur according to package directions.

2. While bulgur is cooking, cut chicken tenders into 1-inch pieces. Heat olive oil in medium skillet. Add chicken; cook and stir until no longer pink in center. Remove from heat; cool slightly.

3. Combine cooked bulgur, chicken, tomato, parsley, green onions and lemon juice in large bowl; toss gently to blend. Season with salt, if desired, and pepper to taste.

makes 4 servings

Prep & Cook Time: 20 minutes

NUTRIENTS PER SERVING

Calories:	249	Carbohydrate:	33g
Calories from Fat:	16%	Fiber:	8g
Total Fat:	5g	Protein:	22g
Saturated Fat:	1g	Sodium:	236mg
Cholesterol:	36mg		

Dietary Exchanges: 2 Starch, 2 Lean Meat

Penne Primavera Salad

- 1 pound penne or medium pasta shells, cooked and cooled
- 1 large yellow or red bell pepper, sliced
- ½ cup fresh or thawed frozen peas, cooked
- ½ cup sliced green onions
- ½ cup blanched sugar snap peas
- ½ cup sliced carrots
- 1 cup skim milk
- ½ cup fat-free mayonnaise
- ½ cup red wine vinegar
- ¼ cup minced parsley
- 2 teaspoons drained green peppercorns, crushed (optional)
- 1¾ teaspoons EQUAL® FOR RECIPES *or* 6 packets EQUAL® sweetener *or* ¼ cup EQUAL® SPOONFUL™
- Salt and pepper

• Combine pasta, bell pepper, peas, green onions, snap peas and carrots in salad bowl. Blend milk and mayonnaise in medium bowl until smooth. Stir in vinegar, parsley, peppercorns and Equal®.

• Pour dressing over salad and toss to coat; season to taste with salt and pepper. *makes 6 servings*

NUTRIENTS PER SERVING

1 cup = 1 serving

Calories:	345	Carbohydrate:	68g
Calories from Fat:	4%	Fiber:	5g
Total Fat:	2g	Protein:	13g
Saturated Fat:	<1g	Sodium:	179mg
Cholesterol:	1mg		

Dietary Exchanges: 4 Starch, 2 Vegetable

recipe tip

Blanch vegetables by boiling them briefly in water and then quickly cooling them in cold water. Blanching the sugar snap peas in this recipe brings out their bright green color, contributing to the dish's overall appeal.

Paella Salad

- 2 cups cooked rice (cooked in chicken broth and ⅛ teaspoon saffron*)
- 1 cup cooked chicken breast cubes
- 1 cup peeled, deveined cooked shrimp
- 1 medium tomato, seeded and diced
- ½ cup chopped onion
- ⅓ cup cooked green peas
- ⅓ cup sliced ripe olives
- 3 tablespoons white wine vinegar
- 1 tablespoon olive oil
- 1 clove garlic, minced
- ½ teaspoon salt
- ½ teaspoon ground white pepper
- Lettuce leaves

**Substitute ground turmeric for the saffron, if desired.*

Combine rice, chicken, shrimp, tomato, onion, peas, and olives in large bowl. Combine vinegar, oil, garlic, salt, and pepper in jar with lid. Pour over rice mixture; toss lightly. Serve on lettuce leaves. *makes 4 servings*

Favorite recipe from **USA Rice Federation**

NUTRIENTS PER SERVING

Calories:	280	Carbohydrate:	26g
Calories from Fat:	33%	Fiber:	2g
Total Fat:	10g	Protein:	21g
Saturated Fat:	2g	Sodium:	1141mg
Cholesterol:	85mg		

Dietary Exchanges: 2 Starch, 2 Lean Meat, ½ Fat

Tip

While this salad is higher in fat, it can still be part of a light meal plan. Just plan your other meals around it.

Green Beans with Savory Mushroom Sauce

- 2 packages (10 ounces each) frozen French-style green beans, thawed
- 1 can (10¾ ounces) condensed cream of mushroom soup, undiluted
- 4 ounces (1½ cups) mushrooms, sliced
- ¼ cup dry vermouth or dry white wine
- ½ teaspoon salt
- ½ teaspoon dried thyme leaves
- ¼ teaspoon black pepper
- 1 cup crushed prepared croutons or canned fried onion rings

SLOW COOKER DIRECTIONS

Combine all ingredients except croutons in slow cooker. Mix until well blended. Cover and cook on LOW 3 to 4 hours or until beans are crisp-tender. Sprinkle with croutons. Serve warm. *makes 6 to 8 servings*

NUTRIENTS PER SERVING

Calories:	116	Carbohydrate:	13g
Calories from Fat:	34%	Fiber:	3g
Total Fat:	4g	Protein:	3g
Saturated Fat:	1g	Sodium:	593mg
Cholesterol:	1mg		

Dietary Exchanges: 3 Vegetable, 1 Fat

Glazed Fruit Kabobs

2 fresh California nectarines, halved, pitted and cut into 6 wedges
3 fresh California plums, halved, pitted and quartered
½ fresh pineapple, peeled and cut into 2-inch cubes
¼ cup packed brown sugar
2 tablespoons water
1½ teaspoons cornstarch
¾ teaspoon rum extract

Alternately thread fruit onto skewers. Combine sugar, water, cornstarch and rum extract in small saucepan. Bring to a boil, stirring constantly, until thickened and clear. Place fruit kabobs in shallow pan. Brush with glaze mixture. (This may be done ahead.) Grill kabobs about 4 to 5 inches from heat 6 to 8 minutes or until hot, turning once, brushing occasionally with glaze.

makes 4 servings

Favorite recipe from **California Tree Fruit Agreement**

NUTRIENTS PER SERVING

Calories:	163	Carbohydrate:	41g
Calories from Fat:	4%	Fiber:	3g
Total Fat:	1g	Protein:	1g
Saturated Fat:	<1g	Sodium:	5mg
Cholesterol:	0mg		

Dietary Exchanges: 2½ Fruit

recipe tip

Here's the best way to prepare a pineapple: First, twist off the crown. Then, using a chef's knife, cut the pineapple lengthwise into halves and then into quarters. Trim off the pineapple's ends and remove the core. Carefully run the blade of a utility knife between the shell and the fruit to remove the fruit. Then cut the fruit into chunks.

Angelic Deviled Eggs

- 6 large eggs
- ¼ cup low-fat (1%) cottage cheese
- 3 tablespoons prepared fat-free Ranch dressing
- 2 teaspoons Dijon mustard
- 2 tablespoons minced fresh chives or dill
- 1 tablespoon diced well-drained pimiento or roasted red pepper

1. Place eggs in medium saucepan; add enough water to cover. Bring to a boil over medium heat. Remove from heat; cover. Let stand 20 minutes. Drain. Add cold water to eggs in saucepan; let stand until eggs are cool. Drain. Remove shells from eggs.

2. Cut eggs lengthwise in half. Remove yolks, reserving 3 yolk halves. Discard remaining yolks or reserve for another use. Place egg whites, cut sides up, on serving plate; cover with plastic wrap. Refrigerate while preparing filling.

3. Combine cottage cheese, dressing, mustard and reserved yolk halves in mini food processor; process until smooth. (Or, place in small bowl and mash with fork until well blended.) Transfer cheese mixture to small bowl; stir in chives and pimiento. Spoon into egg whites. Cover and chill at least 1 hour. Garnish, if desired.

makes 12 servings

NUTRIENTS PER SERVING

1 filled egg half = 1 serving

Calories:	24	Carbohydrate:	1g
Calories from Fat:	26%	Fiber:	1g
Total Fat:	1g	Protein:	3g
Saturated Fat:	<1g	Sodium:	96mg
Cholesterol:	27mg		

Dietary Exchanges: ½ Lean Meat

Savory Lemon Potato Wedges

1½ pounds unpeeled potatoes (about 4 medium), cut lengthwise into 6 wedges
Juice of 1 SUNKIST® lemon (3 tablespoons), divided
1 medium clove garlic, minced
¼ cup sliced green onions
2 tablespoons 50% less fat margarine
Grated peel of ½ lemon
½ teaspoon dried dill weed

In covered non-stick skillet, cook potatoes in gently boiling water with 2 tablespoons lemon juice and garlic 17 to 20 minutes or until tender. *(Do not overcook.)* Drain well. In same skillet, sauté green onions in margarine with lemon peel and dill. Add potatoes and remaining 1 tablespoon lemon juice; heat. *makes 4 servings*

NUTRIENTS PER SERVING

Calories:	173	Carbohydrate:	35g
Calories from Fat:	15%	Fiber:	3g
Total Fat:	3g	Protein:	3g
Saturated Fat:	1g	Sodium:	77mg
Cholesterol:	0mg		

Dietary Exchanges: 2 Starch, ½ Fat

Bean & Spinach Soup

2 cups torn spinach leaves
1½ cups undrained canned cannellini beans
1 cup canned vegetable or chicken broth
⅓ cup thinly sliced carrots
2 tablespoons white wine
1 clove garlic, minced
⅛ teaspoon salt
⅛ teaspoon red pepper flakes

Combine all ingredients in medium saucepan. Bring to a boil. Reduce heat and simmer 15 minutes or until carrots are tender. *makes 2 servings*

NUTRIENTS PER SERVING

Calories:	218	Carbohydrate:	39g
Calories from Fat:	5%	Fiber:	11g
Total Fat:	1g	Protein:	11g
Saturated Fat:	<1g	Sodium:	1079mg
Cholesterol:	0mg		

Dietary Exchanges: 2 Starch, 1 Vegetable, 1 Lean Meat

Confetti Black Beans

1 cup dried black beans
3 cups water
1 can (14 ounces) ⅓-less-sodium chicken broth
1 bay leaf
1½ teaspoons olive oil
1 medium onion, chopped
¼ cup chopped red bell pepper
¼ cup chopped yellow bell pepper
2 cloves garlic, minced
1 jalapeño pepper,* finely chopped
1 large tomato, seeded and chopped
½ teaspoon salt
⅛ teaspoon black pepper
Hot pepper sauce (optional)

**Jalapeño peppers can sting and irritate the skin; wear rubber gloves when handling peppers and do not touch eyes. Wash hands after handling peppers.*

1. Sort and rinse black beans. Cover with water and soak overnight; drain. Place beans in large saucepan with chicken broth; bring to a boil over high heat. Add bay leaf. Reduce heat to low; cover and simmer about 1½ hours or until beans are tender.

2. Heat oil in large skillet over medium heat. Add onion, bell peppers, garlic and jalapeño; cook 8 to 10 minutes or until onion is tender, stirring frequently. Add tomato, salt and black pepper; cook 5 minutes.

3. Add onion mixture to beans; cook 15 to 20 minutes. Remove bay leaf before serving. Serve with hot sauce and garnish, if desired.

makes 6 servings

NUTRIENTS PER SERVING

Calories:	146	Carbohydrate:	24g
Calories from Fat:	14%	Fiber:	6g
Total Fat:	2g	Protein:	8g
Saturated Fat:	<1g	Sodium:	209mg
Cholesterol:	0mg		

Dietary Exchanges: 1½ Starch, ½ Lean Meat, ½ Fat

Cream of Broccoli and Cheese Soup

Nonstick cooking spray
1 cup chopped onion
3 cloves garlic, minced
3 tablespoons all-purpose flour
4 cans (14 ounces each) fat-free reduced-sodium chicken broth
1½ pounds fresh broccoli, chopped
1½ pounds baking potatoes, peeled and cubed
½ cup fat-free (skim) milk, divided
1 cup (4 ounces) shredded reduced-fat Cheddar cheese
½ teaspoon salt
¼ teaspoon white pepper
Ground nutmeg (optional)

1. Spray 4-quart Dutch oven or large saucepan with cooking spray; heat over medium heat. Add onion and garlic and cook until tender. Add flour; stir over low heat 1 to 2 minutes.

2. Add chicken broth; bring to a boil. Add broccoli and potatoes; reduce heat and simmer, covered, about 15 minutes or until vegetables are tender. Remove 1½ cups broccoli mixture with slotted spoon and reserve.

3. Process remaining broccoli mixture in batches in food processor or blender until smooth; return to Dutch oven. Stir in reserved broccoli mixture and milk. Cook over medium heat until heated through. Remove from heat; stir in cheese until melted. Stir in salt and pepper. Sprinkle with ground nutmeg, if desired. *makes 8 servings*

NUTRIENTS PER SERVING

1½ cups soup = 1 serving

Calories:	168	Carbohydrate:	26g
Calories from Fat:	16%	Fiber:	0g
Total Fat:	3g	Protein:	10g
Saturated Fat:	1g	Sodium:	413mg
Cholesterol:	8mg		

Dietary Exchanges: 1 Starch, 2 Vegetable, ½ Lean Meat, ½ Fat

Risotto with Peas and Mushrooms

½ cup chopped onion
2 teaspoons margarine
1 cup uncooked rice
⅓ cup dry white wine
1 cup chicken broth
4 cups water
1 cup frozen peas, thawed
1 jar (2½ ounces) sliced mushrooms, drained
¼ cup grated Parmesan cheese
¼ teaspoon ground white pepper
⅓ cup 2% low-fat milk

Cook onion in margarine in large skillet over medium-high heat until soft. Add rice; stir 2 to 3 minutes. Add wine; stir until absorbed. Stir in broth. Cook, uncovered, stirring constantly, until broth is absorbed. Continue stirring and adding water, one cup at a time; allow each cup to be absorbed before adding another, until rice is tender and has a creamy consistency, 20 to 25 minutes. Stir in remaining ingredients. Stir until creamy, 1 to 2 minutes. Serve immediately. *makes 6 servings*

tip: Medium grain rice will yield the best consistency for risottos, but long grain rice can be used.

Favorite recipe from **USA Rice Federation**

NUTRIENTS PER SERVING

Calories:	189	Carbohydrate:	31g
Calories from Fat:	15%	Fiber:	2g
Total Fat:	3g	Protein:	6g
Saturated Fat:	1g	Sodium:	326mg
Cholesterol:	4mg		

Dietary Exchanges: 2 Starch, 1 Fat

Sweet Potato Pancakes

¼ cup all-purpose flour
½ teaspoon dried rosemary leaves, crushed
⅛ to ¼ teaspoon ground black pepper
2 small sweet potatoes, peeled and shredded (about 3 cups)
1 cup EGG BEATERS® Healthy Real Egg Product
⅓ cup chopped onion
1 tablespoon FLEISCHMANN'S® Original Margarine, divided
Fat-free sour cream or yogurt, optional

In small bowl, combine flour, rosemary and pepper; set aside.

Pat shredded potatoes dry with paper towels. In medium bowl, combine potatoes, Egg Beaters® and onion; stir in flour mixture. In large nonstick skillet, over medium-low heat, melt 2 teaspoons margarine. For each pancake, spoon about ⅓ cup potato mixture into skillet, spreading into a 4-inch circle. Cook for 5 minutes on each side or until golden; remove and keep warm. Repeat with remaining mixture, using remaining margarine as needed to make 8 pancakes. Serve hot with sour cream or yogurt, if desired. *makes 8 pancakes*

Prep Time: 15 minutes
Cook Time: 20 minutes

NUTRIENTS PER SERVING

2 (4-inch) pancakes without sour cream = 1 serving

Calories:	109	Carbohydrate:	20g
Calories from Fat:	11%	Fiber:	1g
Total Fat:	1g	Protein:	5g
Saturated Fat:	<1g	Sodium:	68mg
Cholesterol:	0mg		

Dietary Exchanges: 1 Starch, ½ Fat

Two Beans and Rice

- 1½ cups chopped onion
- 1 cup chopped green bell pepper
- 1 cup thinly sliced celery
- 2 cloves garlic, minced
- 1 teaspoon olive oil
- 2 cups chopped seeded tomatoes
- 1 can (15½ ounces) reduced-sodium kidney beans, rinsed, drained and slightly mashed
- 1 can (15 ounces) black beans, rinsed, drained and slightly mashed
- ¼ cup water
- 1 bay leaf
- ½ teaspoon chicken bouillon granules
- ¼ teaspoon ground red pepper
- 4 cups hot cooked brown or white rice
- ¼ cup reduced-fat sour cream
- ¼ cup chopped fresh cilantro or parsley

Spray 3-quart saucepan with nonstick cooking spray; heat saucepan over medium heat. Cook and stir onion, bell pepper, celery and garlic in oil until vegetables are tender.

Stir in tomatoes, kidney beans, black beans, water, bay leaf, bouillon and red pepper. Bring to a boil over high heat. Reduce heat to medium-low. Simmer 15 minutes, stirring occasionally. Remove bay leaf. Serve bean mixture over rice. Top with sour cream and sprinkle with cilantro.

makes 4 servings

NUTRIENTS PER SERVING

Calories:	507	Carbohydrate:	98g
Calories from Fat:	11%	Fiber:	19g
Total Fat:	6g	Protein:	23g
Saturated Fat:	1g	Sodium:	517mg
Cholesterol:	6mg		

Dietary Exchanges: 5½ Starch, 3 Vegetable, 1 Fat

Brown rice is more nutritious than white rice because it contains the bran and the germ of the rice kernel, making it higher in fiber, B vitamins and several essential minerals.

Apple Raisin Risotto

3 tablespoons margarine, divided
1 large Golden Delicious apple, peeled, cored and diced
¾ cup arborio rice
⅓ cup raisins
¼ cup frozen unsweetened apple juice concentrate, thawed
1 cup unsweetened apple juice, divided
1 tablespoon firmly packed dark brown sugar
½ teaspoon ground cinnamon
1 can (12 ounces) evaporated skimmed milk
1½ cups fat-free (skim) milk
1½ teaspoons vanilla

1. Melt 2 tablespoons margarine in large, heavy saucepan over medium heat. Add apple. Cook and stir until apple can be easily pierced with fork. Add rice; stir until grains become shiny. Add raisins and apple juice concentrate. Cook and stir until all of concentrate is absorbed.

2. Add ½ cup apple juice. Cook and stir until most of juice is absorbed. Add remaining ½ cup apple juice. Cook and stir until most of juice is absorbed. Add brown sugar and cinnamon; mix well. Reduce heat to low.

3. Combine evaporated skimmed milk and skim milk in medium saucepan. Heat over medium heat just until mixture becomes warm. Do not boil. Remove from heat.

4. Add ½ cup milk mixture to rice mixture. Cook and stir until most of milk is absorbed; repeat until all milk mixture is used. Do not allow last addition of milk to be completely absorbed. Remove from heat. Stir in remaining 1 tablespoon margarine and vanilla. Serve immediately. *makes 8 servings*

NUTRIENTS PER SERVING

½ cup = 1 serving

Calories:	218	Carbohydrate:	38g
Calories from Fat:	19%	Fiber:	1g
Total Fat:	5g	Protein:	6g
Saturated Fat:	1g	Sodium:	127mg
Cholesterol:	2mg		

Dietary Exchanges: 1 Starch, 1 Fruit, ½ Milk, 1 Fat

Mediterranean Baked Potato Topper

- ½ cup chopped red bell pepper
- ¼ cup part-skim ricotta cheese
- ¼ cup reduced-fat sour cream
- 1 large clove garlic, crushed
- 1 teaspoon dried basil leaves
- ¼ teaspoon salt
- ¼ teaspoon black pepper
- ½ cup chopped and seeded plum tomato
- 4 large hot baked potatoes, cut into halves

Combine bell pepper, cheese, sour cream, garlic, basil, salt and pepper in small bowl. Mix well. Add tomatoes. Toss gently. Cover and refrigerate at least 2 hours. To serve, spoon topping over potato halves.

makes 8 servings

NUTRIENTS PER SERVING

Calories:	98	Carbohydrate:	20g
Calories from Fat:	12%	Fiber:	2g
Total Fat:	1g	Protein:	3g
Saturated Fat:	1g	Sodium:	93mg
Cholesterol:	5mg		

Dietary Exchanges: 1 Starch, 1 Vegetable

Quick Creamed Cauliflower

- 1 package (10 ounces) frozen cauliflower
- ½ cup chicken broth, defatted
- ½ cup evaporated skimmed milk
- 2 tablespoons all-purpose flour
- Salt and pepper to taste (optional)
- Paprika (optional)

Combine cauliflower and chicken broth in saucepan. Simmer, covered, 10 to 12 minutes or until cauliflower is tender. Combine milk and flour; mix well. Stir into saucepan. Cook and stir until sauce simmers and bubbles. Sprinkle with salt, pepper and paprika, if desired, before serving.

makes 3 servings

NUTRIENTS PER SERVING

Calories:	74	Carbohydrate:	13g
Calories from Fat:	6%	Fiber:	2g
Total Fat:	1g	Protein:	6g
Saturated Fat:	<1g	Sodium:	122mg
Cholesterol:	2mg		

Dietary Exchanges: ½ Milk, 1 Vegetable

Grilled Balsamic-Herb Ratatouille

2 tablespoons balsamic vinegar
1 tablespoon olive oil
Balsamic-Herb Vinaigrette (recipe on page 296)
2 yellow or red bell peppers, seeded and halved
1 medium eggplant (about 1 pound)
1 small onion, peeled and quartered
12 mushrooms
2 small yellow zucchini, halved lengthwise
½ pint cherry tomatoes
⅓ cup slivered fresh basil

1. Prepare coals for grilling. Spray medium casserole with nonstick cooking spray; set aside. To make basting mixture, combine vinegar and oil in small bowl; set aside. Prepare Balsamic-Herb Vinaigrette.

2. Grill bell pepper halves skin-side down on covered grill over hot coals 15 to 25 minutes or until skin is charred. Place in plastic bag 10 minutes. Remove skin and discard. Dice bell peppers; place in casserole and keep warm.

3. Slice eggplant into ½-inch-thick rounds. Thread onion quarters onto metal skewers. Baste eggplant and onion; grill on covered grill over medium coals 20 to 30 minutes or until tender, basting and turning every 10 minutes. Cut eggplant into ½-inch strips. Add onion and eggplant to casserole.

4. Thread mushrooms onto metal skewers. Baste mushrooms and cut sides of zucchini. Grill mushrooms and zucchini on covered grill over medium coals 10 to 15 minutes or until tender, basting and turning once. Cut zucchini into ½-inch slices. Add mushrooms and zucchini to casserole. Thread tomatoes onto skewers. Grill on covered grill over medium coals 5 minutes or until blistered, basting and turning once. Add to casserole. Stir in Balsamic-Herb Vinaigrette and basil.

makes 6 servings

continued on page 296

Balsamic-Herb Vinaigrette

4 cloves garlic, minced
3 tablespoons balsamic vinegar
1 teaspoon dried oregano leaves *or* 1 tablespoon minced fresh oregano
1 teaspoon dried thyme leaves *or* 1 tablespoon minced fresh thyme
1 teaspoon Dijon mustard
½ teaspoon black pepper

Whisk together all ingredients in small bowl; set aside.

makes about ¼ cup

NUTRIENTS PER SERVING

Calories:	105	Carbohydrate:	19g
Calories from Fat:	23%	Fiber:	4g
Total Fat:	3g	Protein:	3g
Saturated Fat:	<1g	Sodium:	22mg
Cholesterol:	<1mg		

Dietary Exchanges: 3 Vegetable, ½ Fat

Rigatoni with Broccoli

- 8 ounces uncooked rigatoni pasta
- 1 bunch fresh broccoli, trimmed and separated into florets with 1-inch stems
- 1 tablespoon FILIPPO BERIO® Extra Virgin Olive Oil
- 1 clove garlic, minced
- Crushed red pepper
- Grated Parmesan cheese

Cook pasta according to package directions until al dente (tender but still firm). Add broccoli during last 5 minutes of cooking time; cook until broccoli is tender-crisp. Drain pasta and broccoli; transfer to large bowl. Meanwhile, in small skillet, heat olive oil over medium heat until hot. Add garlic; cook and stir 1 to 2 minutes or until golden. Pour oil mixture over hot pasta mixture; toss until lightly coated. Season to taste with pepper. Top with cheese.

makes 3 to 4 servings

NUTRIENTS PER SERVING

Calories:	288	Carbohydrate:	42g
Calories from Fat:	25%	Fiber:	2g
Total Fat:	8g	Protein:	13g
Saturated Fat:	1g	Sodium:	55mg
Cholesterol:	99mg		

Dietary Exchanges: 2 Starch, 2 Vegetable, 2 Fat

recipe tip

Wondering what rigatoni looks like? It's the large, grooved, tube-shaped pasta—about 1½ inches wide.

Wild Rice and Lentil Pilaf

- 4½ cups water, divided
- ¾ cup dried brown lentils, sorted, rinsed and drained
- Nonstick cooking spray
- 1 tablespoon plus 2 teaspoons extra-virgin olive oil, divided
- 2 cups finely chopped yellow onions
- 1 medium red bell pepper, chopped
- 1 cup thinly sliced celery
- 4 cloves garlic, minced
- ½ teaspoon dried oregano leaves
- ½ teaspoon salt
- Dash ground red pepper (optional)
- 1 box (6.2-ounce) quick-cooking white and wild rice with seasoning packet

Bring 4 cups water to a boil in medium saucepan. Stir in lentils and return to a boil. Reduce heat to low and simmer, uncovered, 10 minutes.

Meanwhile, heat large nonstick skillet over medium-high heat until hot. Coat skillet with cooking spray. Add 2 teaspoons oil and tilt skillet to coat bottom evenly. Add onions, bell pepper, celery, garlic and oregano; cook 12 minutes or until celery is crisp-tender, stirring frequently. Stir in remaining ½ cup water, salt and ground red pepper, if desired.

When lentils have cooked 10 minutes, stir in rice and seasoning packet. Cover tightly and simmer 5 minutes. Remove from heat. Stir in onion mixture and remaining 1 tablespoon oil; toss gently. *makes 7 servings*

variation: For a more decorative dish, coat a 6-cup mold with cooking spray. Place rice mixture in mold and press down gently but firmly to allow rice mixture to stick together. Place a dinner plate on top of mold and invert mold onto plate. Tap gently on side and top of mold to release rice mixture and slowly remove mold. Garnish with red bell pepper cutouts or strips.

NUTRIENTS PER SERVING

1 cup = 1 serving

Calories:	205	Carbohydrate:	35g
Calories from Fat:	18%	Fiber:	6g
Total Fat:	4g	Protein:	8g
Saturated Fat:	<1g	Sodium:	556mg
Cholesterol:	2mg		

Dietary Exchanges: 2 Starch, 1 Vegetable, 1 Fat

Santa Fe Fusilli

- 1 medium red bell pepper*
- 2 teaspoons cumin seeds
- ¾ cup chopped, seeded tomato
- ¼ cup chopped onion
- 1 clove garlic, minced
- 1 tablespoon chili powder
- ¼ teaspoon red pepper flakes
- ¼ teaspoon black pepper
- 1 can (16 ounces) no-salt-added tomato purée
- ⅓ cup water
- 1 teaspoon sugar
- 8 ounces uncooked fusilli pasta
- 1 can (16 ounces) black beans, rinsed and drained
- 1 package (10 ounces) frozen corn, thawed and drained
- 1 can (4 ounces) diced green chilies, drained
- ⅓ cup low-fat sour cream
- Fresh cilantro

**Or, substitute 1 jar (7 ounces) roasted peppers.*

1. Roast bell pepper over charcoal or gas flame or place under broiler, turning several times, until skin is charred. Cool 10 minutes. Peel and discard charred skin. Cut pepper in half; seed, devein and coarsely chop. Set aside.

2. Place cumin seeds in large nonstick saucepan; cook and stir over medium heat until lightly toasted, about 3 minutes. Stir in tomato, onion, garlic, chili powder, red pepper flakes and black pepper; cook until onion is tender, about 5 minutes. Stir in tomato purée, water and sugar. Reduce heat to low; simmer, covered, 15 minutes.

3. Cook pasta according to package directions, omitting salt. Drain; set aside. Stir beans, corn, roasted peppers and chilies into vegetable mixture; cook until heated through, about 8 minutes. Stir in pasta; top with sour cream and cilantro.

makes 8 servings

NUTRIENTS PER SERVING

Calories:	228	Carbohydrate:	46g
Calories from Fat:	9%	Fiber:	8g
Total Fat:	2g	Protein:	12g
Saturated Fat:	<1g	Sodium:	215mg
Cholesterol:	3mg		

Dietary Exchanges: 2 Starch, 2½ Vegetable, ½ Lean Meat

Potatoes au Gratin

1 pound baking potatoes
4 teaspoons reduced-fat margarine
4 teaspoons all-purpose flour
1¼ cups fat-free (skim) milk
¼ teaspoon ground nutmeg
¼ teaspoon paprika
Pinch white pepper
½ cup thinly sliced red onion, divided
⅓ cup whole wheat bread crumbs
1 tablespoon finely chopped red onion
1 tablespoon grated Parmesan cheese

1. Spray 4- or 6-cup casserole with nonstick cooking spray; set aside.

2. Place potatoes in large saucepan; add water to cover. Bring to a boil over high heat. Boil 12 minutes or until potatoes are tender. Drain; let potatoes stand 10 minutes or until cool enough to handle.

3. Melt margarine in small saucepan over medium heat. Add flour. Cook and stir 3 minutes or until small clumps form. Gradually whisk in milk. Cook 8 minutes or until sauce thickens, stirring constantly. Remove saucepan from heat. Stir in nutmeg, paprika and pepper.

4. Preheat oven to 350°F. Cut potatoes into thin slices. Arrange half of potato slices in prepared casserole. Sprinkle with half of onion slices. Repeat layers. Spoon sauce over potato mixture. Combine bread crumbs, finely chopped red onion and cheese in small bowl. Sprinkle mixture evenly over sauce.

5. Bake 20 minutes. Let stand 5 minutes before serving. Garnish as desired.

makes 4 servings

NUTRIENTS PER SERVING

Calories: 178
Calories from Fat: ..14%
Total Fat: 3g
Saturated Fat: 1g
Cholesterol: 2mg
Carbohydrate: 33g
Fiber: 2g
Protein: 6g
Sodium: 144mg

Dietary Exchanges: 2 Starch, ½ Vegetable, ½ Fat

Sinless Sweets

Brownies

- ½ cup boiling water
- ½ cup unsweetened cocoa powder
- 1¼ cups all-purpose flour
- ¾ cup granulated sugar
- ¾ cup firmly packed light brown sugar
- 1 teaspoon baking powder
- ¼ teaspoon salt
- 4 egg whites, lightly beaten
- ⅓ cup vegetable oil
- 1½ teaspoons vanilla
- ½ cup chopped unsalted mixed nuts (optional)

1. Preheat oven to 350°F.

2. Spray 13×9-inch baking pan with nonstick cooking spray. Combine boiling water and cocoa in large bowl. Mix until completely dissolved. Add flour, granulated sugar, brown sugar, baking powder, salt, egg whites, oil and vanilla; mix well. Fold in chopped nuts, if desired.

3. Pour mixture into prepared pan. Bake 25 minutes or until brownies spring back when lightly touched. Do not overbake. Cool in pan on wire rack; cut into squares.

makes 32 brownies

NUTRIENTS PER SERVING

1 brownie without nuts = 1 serving

Calories: 81	Carbohydrate: 14g
Calories from Fat: ..26%	Fiber: 0g
Total Fat: 2g	Protein: 1g
Saturated Fat: .....<1g	Sodium: 37mg
Cholesterol: 0mg	

Dietary Exchanges: 1 Starch, ½ Fat

Carrot Raisin Spice Cookies

- 1¼ cups all-purpose flour
- ½ cup CREAM OF WHEAT® Cereal (1-minute, 2½-minute or 10-minute stovetop cooking)
- 1½ teaspoons ground cinnamon
- 1 teaspoon pumpkin pie spice
- ¾ teaspoon baking soda
- ½ cup margarine or butter, softened
- ½ cup granulated sugar
- ⅓ cup packed light brown sugar
- ¼ cup egg substitute
- 1 teaspoon vanilla extract
- ½ cup finely grated carrot
- ½ cup seedless raisins
- ¼ cup PLANTERS® Walnuts, finely chopped
- Powdered sugar glaze, optional

1. Mix flour, cereal, cinnamon, pumpkin pie spice and baking soda in medium bowl; set aside.

2. Beat margarine or butter and sugars in large bowl with mixer until creamy; beat in egg substitute and vanilla.

3. Reduce speed to low; blend in flour mixture.

4. Stir in carrot, raisins and walnuts; let stand 10 minutes.

5. Drop by teaspoonfuls 2 inches apart onto lightly greased baking sheets.

6. Bake at 350°F for 10 to 12 minutes or until golden brown. Cool on wire racks. Drizzle with powdered sugar glaze, if desired. *makes 2½ dozen cookies*

NUTRIENTS PER SERVING

1 cookie without glaze = 1 serving

Calories:	88	Carbohydrate:	13g
Calories from Fat:	36%	Fiber:	<1g
Total Fat:	4g	Protein:	1g
Saturated Fat:	1g	Sodium:	72mg
Cholesterol:	0mg		

Dietary Exchanges: 1 Starch, ½ Fat

Butterscotch Bars

- ¾ cup all-purpose flour
- ½ cup packed brown sugar
- ½ cup fat-free butterscotch ice cream topping
- ¼ cup cholesterol-free egg substitute
- 3 tablespoons margarine or butter, melted
- 1 teaspoon vanilla
- ¼ teaspoon salt
- ½ cup toasted chopped pecans (optional)

1. Preheat oven to 350°F. Lightly coat 8-inch square baking pan with nonstick cooking spray; set aside.

2. Combine all ingredients in medium bowl; stir until blended. Spread into prepared pan.

3. Bake 15 to 18 minutes or until firm to touch. Cool completely in pan. Cut into 16 bars. *makes 16 bars*

NUTRIENTS PER SERVING

1 bar = 1 serving

Calories:	95	Carbohydrate:	18g
Calories from Fat:	20%	Fiber:	<1g
Total Fat:	2g	Protein:	1g
Saturated Fat:	<1g	Sodium:	107mg
Cholesterol:	<1mg		

Dietary Exchanges: 1 Starch, ½ Fat

recipe tip

If you plan to include pecans in this recipe, preheat your oven to 350°F. Spread the nuts in a single layer on a baking sheet and toast them for 8 to 10 minutes.

Nutty Spice Cookies

½ cup light molasses
⅓ cup sugar
¼ cup egg substitute
¼ cup water
2 tablespoons canola or vegetable oil
2¼ cups all-purpose flour
1 teaspoon baking soda
1 teaspoon ground ginger
½ teaspoon ground nutmeg
½ teaspoon ground cinnamon
¼ teaspoon ground cloves
⅓ cup chopped walnuts

Spray cookie sheets lightly with nonstick cooking spray; set aside. Stir molasses, sugar, egg substitute, water and oil in medium bowl until sugar is dissolved. Sift flour, baking soda, ginger, nutmeg, cinnamon and cloves into large bowl; stir to combine. Add molasses mixture; stir with wooden spoon until smooth. (Dough will be stiff.) Refrigerate, covered, at least 2 hours or up to 2 days.

Preheat oven to 375°F. Roll out dough into 12-inch square on floured surface. If dough cracks, press together. Sprinkle walnuts evenly over dough, pressing nuts into dough with fingers. Cut square into 8 lengthwise strips and then 8 crosswise strips to form 64 squares.

Place cookies 1 inch apart on prepared cookie sheets. Bake, 1 sheet at a time, 8 minutes or until edges begin to brown. Remove cookies to wire racks; cool completely. Store in airtight container. *makes 64 cookies*

NUTRIENTS PER SERVING

Calories:	34	Carbohydrate:	6g
Calories from Fat:	20%	Fiber:	<1g
Total Fat:	1g	Protein:	1g
Saturated Fat:	<1g	Sodium:	15mg
Cholesterol:	0mg		

Dietary Exchanges: ½ Starch

Frosted Sugar Cookies, continued

NUTRIENTS PER SERVING

1 cookie = 1 serving

Calories:	44	Carbohydrate:	7g
Calories from Fat:	28%	Fiber:	0g
Total Fat:	1g	Protein:	0g
Saturated Fat:	0g	Sodium:	34mg
Cholesterol:	0mg		

Dietary Exchanges: ½ Starch

Quick Chocolate Chip Cookie Cakes

- 1 package (18.25 ounces) reduced-fat yellow cake mix
- ½ cup cholesterol-free egg substitute
- ¼ cup vegetable oil
- ¼ cup reduced-fat sour cream
- 2 cups uncooked old-fashioned oats
- ½ cup reduced-fat semisweet chocolate chips

1. Preheat oven to 350°F. Lightly coat cookie sheet with nonstick cooking spray; set aside.

2. Combine cake mix, egg substitute, oil and sour cream in medium bowl. Add oats and chocolate chips.

3. Drop dough by teaspoonfuls onto prepared cookie sheet.

4. Bake 12 minutes or until lightly browned. Remove to wire rack; cool completely.

makes 4 dozen cookies

NUTRIENTS PER SERVING

1 cookie = 1 serving

Calories:	79	Carbohydrate:	13g
Calories from Fat:	29%	Fiber:	<1g
Total Fat:	3g	Protein:	1g
Saturated Fat:	1g	Sodium:	74mg
Cholesterol:	<1mg		

Dietary Exchanges: 1 Starch

Granola Bites

- 2 cups cornflakes cereal
- ⅔ cup quick-cooking oats
- ¼ cup 100% bran cereal
- ½ cup chopped pitted dates or raisins
- ½ cup reduced-fat crunchy peanut butter
- 4 egg whites *or* ½ cup real liquid egg product
- 5 teaspoons EQUAL® FOR RECIPES *or* 16 packets EQUAL® sweetener *or* ⅔ cup EQUAL® SPOONFUL™
- 2 teaspoons vanilla

• Combine cornflakes, oats, bran cereal and dates in large bowl. Mix peanut butter, egg whites, Equal® and vanilla in small bowl until smooth; pour over cereal mixture and stir until all ingredients are coated.

• Shape mixture into 1-inch mounds; place on lightly greased cookie sheets. Bake in preheated 350°F oven until cookies are set and browned, 8 to 10 minutes. Cool on wire racks. *makes about 2 dozen*

NUTRIENTS PER SERVING

1 cookie = 1 serving

Calories:	66	Carbohydrate:	9g
Calories from Fat:	29%	Fiber:	1g
Total Fat:	2g	Protein:	3g
Saturated Fat:	<1g	Sodium:	70mg
Cholesterol:	0mg		

Dietary Exchanges: ½ Starch, ½ Fat

Cookies for breakfast? These Granola Bites are a healthy way to satisfy an early morning craving for sweets.

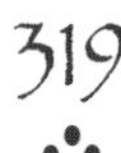

No-Bake Pineapple Marmalade Squares

- 1 cup graham cracker crumbs
- ½ cup plus 2 tablespoons sugar, divided
- ¼ cup light margarine, melted
- 1 cup fat free or light sour cream
- 4 ounces light cream cheese, softened
- ¼ cup orange marmalade or apricot fruit spread, divided
- 1 can (20 ounces) DOLE® Crushed Pineapple
- 1 envelope unflavored gelatin

• Combine graham cracker crumbs, 2 tablespoons sugar and margarine in 8-inch square glass baking dish; pat mixture firmly and evenly onto bottom of dish. Freeze 10 minutes.

• Beat sour cream, cream cheese, remaining ½ cup sugar and 1 tablespoon marmalade in medium bowl until smooth and blended; set aside.

• Drain pineapple; reserve ¼ cup juice.

• Sprinkle gelatin over reserved juice in small saucepan; let stand 1 minute. Cook and stir over low heat until gelatin dissolves.

• Beat gelatin mixture into sour cream mixture until well blended. Spoon mixture evenly over crust.

• Stir together pineapple and remaining 3 tablespoons marmalade in small bowl until blended. Evenly spoon over sour cream filling. Cover and refrigerate 2 hours or until firm.

makes 16 servings

NUTRIENTS PER SERVING

Calories:	146	Carbohydrate:	26g
Calories from Fat:	24%	Fiber:	1g
Total Fat:	4g	Protein:	2g
Saturated Fat:	1g	Sodium:	112mg
Cholesterol:	3mg		

Dietary Exchanges: 1 Starch, ½ Fruit, 1 Fat

Marble Brownies

½ cup plus 2 tablespoons all-purpose flour, divided
½ cup unsweetened cocoa powder
1 teaspoon baking powder
½ teaspoon salt
1¾ cups sugar, divided
2 tablespoons margarine, softened
½ cup MOTT'S® Natural Apple Sauce
3 egg whites, divided
1½ teaspoons vanilla extract, divided
4 ounces low fat cream cheese (Neufchâtel), softened

1. Preheat oven to 350°F. Spray 8-inch square baking pan with nonstick cooking spray.

2. In small bowl, sift together ½ cup flour, cocoa, baking powder and salt.

3. In large bowl, beat 1½ cups sugar and margarine with electric mixer at medium speed until blended. Whisk in apple sauce, 2 egg whites and 1 teaspoon vanilla.

4. Add flour mixture to apple sauce mixture; stir until well blended. Pour batter into prepared pan.

5. In small bowl, beat cream cheese and remaining ¼ cup sugar with electric mixer at medium speed until blended. Stir in remaining egg white, 2 tablespoons flour and ½ teaspoon vanilla. Pour over brownie batter; run knife through batters to marble.

6. Bake 35 to 40 minutes or until firm. Cool on wire rack 15 minutes; cut into 12 bars.

makes 12 servings

NUTRIENTS PER SERVING

1 bar = 1 serving

Calories:	194	Carbohydrate:	37g
Calories from Fat:	19%	Fiber:	<1g
Total Fat:	4g	Protein:	3g
Saturated Fat:	2g	Sodium:	218mg
Cholesterol:	7mg		

Dietary Exchanges: 2 Starch, 1 Fat

Little Fudge and Raisin Cakes

2½ cups all-purpose flour
½ cup unsweetened cocoa powder
1½ teaspoons cinnamon
1 teaspoon baking soda
¼ teaspoon salt
1½ cups firmly packed brown sugar
1 cup unsweetened Michigan Applesauce
¼ cup vegetable oil
2 egg whites
1 teaspoon vanilla
½ cup raisins
Vegetable cooking spray

COFFEE GLAZE

1½ cups powdered sugar
2 tablespoons cold strong coffee

1. Preheat oven to 375°F. Spray baking sheets with nonstick cooking spray; set aside. In small bowl, combine flour, cocoa, cinnamon, baking soda and salt; set aside.

2. In large bowl, beat brown sugar, Michigan Applesauce, oil, egg whites and vanilla; stir in raisins. Add flour mixture, stirring until combined. Drop by slightly rounded tablespoonfuls onto prepared baking sheets.

3. Bake about 8 minutes or until cookies are firm. Remove from baking sheets and place on wire racks. Cool.

4. In small bowl, mix powdered sugar and coffee; drizzle over cooled cookies. Store in airtight container.

makes 3½ dozen cookies

Favorite recipe from **Michigan Apple Committee**

NUTRIENTS PER SERVING

1 cookie = 1 serving

Calories:	96	Carbohydrate:	20g
Calories from Fat:	12%	Fiber:	<1g
Total Fat:	1g	Protein:	1g
Saturated Fat:	<1g	Sodium:	52mg
Cholesterol:	<1mg		

Dietary Exchanges: 1 Starch

Apple-Apricot Bars

- ¾ cups chopped dried apples
- ¾ cup chopped dried apricots
- 3½ teaspoons EQUAL® FOR RECIPES *or* 12 packets EQUAL® sweetener
- 1 cup water
- 5 tablespoons margarine, softened
- 1¾ teaspoons EQUAL® FOR RECIPES *or* 6 packets EQUAL® sweetener
- 1 egg
- 2 egg whites
- 1 teaspoon vanilla
- 1¾ cups all-purpose flour
- ½ teaspoon baking soda
- ¼ teaspoon salt
- Skim milk

• Heat apples, apricots, 3½ teaspoons EQUAL® FOR RECIPES, and water to boiling in small saucepan; reduce heat and simmer, uncovered, until fruit is tender and water is absorbed, about 10 minutes. Process mixture in food processor or blender until smooth; cool.

• Beat margarine and 1¾ teaspoons EQUAL® FOR RECIPES in medium bowl until fluffy; beat in egg, egg whites, and vanilla. Mix in combined flour, baking soda, and salt. Divide dough into 4 equal parts; roll each into a log about 5 inches long. Refrigerate, covered, until firm, about 2 hours.

• Roll 1 piece dough on floured surface into rectangle 12×4 inches. Spread ¼ of the fruit filling in a 1½-inch strip in the center of dough. Fold sides of dough over filling, pressing edges to seal. Cut filled dough in half and place on greased cookie sheet. Repeat with remaining dough and fruit filling.

• Brush top of dough lightly with milk; bake in preheated 400°F oven until lightly browned, 10 to 12 minutes. Remove from pan and cool on wire racks; cut into 1½-inch bars. Store in airtight container.

makes about 2½ dozen bars

NUTRIENTS PER SERVING

Calories:	63	Carbohydrate:	9g
Calories from Fat:	30%	Fiber:	1g
Total Fat:	2g	Protein:	2g
Saturated Fat:	<1g	Sodium:	90mg
Cholesterol:	7mg		

Dietary Exchanges: ½ Starch, ½ Fat

Pumpkin & Chocolate Chip Cookies

2 cups all-purpose flour
1 teaspoon baking soda
1 teaspoon ground cinnamon
½ teaspoon salt
¼ teaspoon ground nutmeg
¼ teaspoon ground cloves
½ cup solid-pack pumpkin
½ cup granulated sugar
½ cup packed brown sugar
¼ cup caramel-flavored low-fat yogurt
1 egg
½ cup mini semisweet chocolate chips

1. Preheat oven to 350°F. Lightly coat cookie sheets with nonstick cooking spray; set aside.

2. Combine flour, baking soda, cinnamon, salt, nutmeg and cloves in medium bowl; set aside.

3. Combine pumpkin, sugars, yogurt and egg in large bowl. Blend in flour mixture. Add chocolate chips.

4. Drop dough by teaspoonfuls onto prepared cookie sheets. Bake 10 minutes or until firm to touch. Remove to wire racks; cool completely. *makes 3 dozen cookies*

NUTRIENTS PER SERVING

1 cookie = 1 serving

Calories:	63	Carbohydrate:	13g
Calories from Fat:	14%	Fiber:	<1g
Total Fat:	1g	Protein:	1g
Saturated Fat:	<1g	Sodium:	72mg
Cholesterol:	6mg		

Dietary Exchanges: 1 Starch

Do Dessert!

Chocolate Mousse

- ½ cup plus 2 tablespoons sugar, divided
- ¼ cup unsweetened cocoa powder
- 1 envelope unflavored gelatin
- 2 tablespoons coffee-flavored liqueur
- 2 cups fat-free (skim) milk
- ¼ cup cholesterol-free egg substitute
- 2 egg whites
- ⅛ teaspoon cream of tartar
- ½ cup thawed frozen reduced-fat nondairy whipped topping

1. Combine ½ cup sugar, cocoa and gelatin in medium saucepan. Add coffee-flavored liqueur; let stand 2 minutes. Add milk; heat over medium heat. Stir until sugar and gelatin are dissolved. Stir in egg substitute. Set aside.

2. Beat egg whites in medium bowl with electric mixer at medium speed until foamy; add cream of tartar. Beat until soft peaks form. Gradually beat in remaining 2 tablespoons sugar; continue beating until stiff peaks form.

3. Gently fold egg whites into cocoa mixture. Fold in whipped topping. Divide evenly between 8 dessert dishes. Refrigerate until thickened. Garnish as desired.

makes 8 servings

NUTRIENTS PER SERVING

Calories:	118	Carbohydrate:	23g
Calories from Fat:	3%	Fiber:	0g
Total Fat:	<1g	Protein:	5g
Saturated Fat:	<1g	Sodium:	60mg
Cholesterol:	1mg		

Dietary Exchanges: 1½ Starch

Tiramisu

⅓ cup GENERAL FOODS INTERNATIONAL COFFEES, Sugar Free Fat Free Suisse Mocha Flavor, divided
2 tablespoons hot water
1 package (3 ounces) ladyfingers, split
2½ cups cold fat-free milk, divided
1 container (8 ounces) PHILADELPHIA FREE® Soft Fat Free Cream Cheese
2 packages (4-serving size each) JELL-O® Vanilla Flavor Fat Free Sugar Free Instant Reduced Calorie Pudding & Pie Filling
1 cup thawed COOL WHIP LITE® Whipped Topping

DISSOLVE 1 tablespoon of the flavored instant coffee in hot water in small bowl.

COVER bottom and sides of shallow 2-quart dessert dish with ladyfingers. Sprinkle dissolved flavored instant coffee over ladyfingers.

PLACE ½ cup of the milk, cream cheese and remaining undissolved flavored instant coffee in blender container; cover. Blend on medium speed until smooth. Add pudding mixes and remaining 2 cups milk; cover. Blend on medium speed until smooth. Carefully pour into prepared bowl. Top with whipped topping.

REFRIGERATE at least 3 hours or until set. Just before serving, sprinkle with additional undissolved flavored instant coffee, if desired. *makes 12 servings*

Prep: 15 minutes plus refrigerating

NUTRIENTS PER SERVING

Calories: 100
Calories from Fat: . .18%
Total Fat: 2g
Saturated Fat: 1g
Cholesterol: 30mg
Carbohydrate: 16g
Fiber: 0g
Protein: 6g
Sodium: 370mg

Dietary Exchanges: 1 Starch, ½ Fat

Creamy Rice Pudding

2 cups water
1 cinnamon stick, broken into pieces
1 cup converted rice
4 cups skim milk
¼ teaspoon salt
7¼ teaspoons EQUAL® FOR RECIPES *or* 24 packets EQUAL® sweetener *or* 1 cup EQUAL® SPOONFUL™
3 egg yolks
2 egg whites
1 teaspoon vanilla
¼ cup raisins
Ground cinnamon and nutmeg

• Heat water and cinnamon stick to boiling in large saucepan; stir in rice. Reduce heat and simmer, covered, until rice is tender and water is absorbed, 20 to 25 minutes. Discard cinnamon stick.

• Stir in milk and salt; heat to boiling. Reduce heat and simmer, covered, until mixture starts to thicken, about 15 to 20 minutes, stirring frequently. (Milk will not be absorbed and pudding will thicken when it cools.) Remove from heat and cool 1 to 2 minutes; stir in Equal®.

• Beat egg yolks, egg whites and vanilla in small bowl until blended. Stir about ½ cup rice mixture into egg mixture; stir back into saucepan. Cook over low heat, stirring constantly, 1 to 2 minutes. Stir in raisins.

• Spoon pudding into serving bowl; sprinkle with cinnamon and nutmeg. Serve warm or at room temperature.

makes 6 (⅔-cup) servings

NUTRIENTS PER SERVING

⅔ cup pudding = 1 serving

Calories:	243	Carbohydrate:	39g
Calories from Fat:	12%	Fiber:	1g
Total Fat:	3g	Protein:	14g
Saturated Fat:	1g	Sodium:	206mg
Cholesterol:	109mg		

Dietary Exchanges: 2 Starch, 1 Milk, ½ Fat

Maple Pumpkin Pie

1⅓ cups all-purpose flour
⅓ cup plus 1 tablespoon sugar, divided
¾ teaspoon salt, divided
2 tablespoons vegetable shortening
2 tablespoons margarine
4 to 5 tablespoons ice water
1 can (15 ounces) solid-pack pumpkin
2 egg whites
1 cup evaporated skimmed milk
⅓ cup maple syrup
1 teaspoon ground cinnamon
½ teaspoon ground ginger
Light nondairy whipped topping (optional)

1. Combine flour, 1 tablespoon sugar and ¼ teaspoon salt in medium bowl. Cut in shortening and margarine with pastry blender or two knives until mixture forms coarse crumbs. Mix in ice water, 1 tablespoon at a time, until mixture comes together and forms a soft dough. Wrap in plastic wrap. Refrigerate 30 minutes.

2. Preheat oven to 425°F. Roll out pastry on floured surface to ⅛-inch thickness. Cut into 12-inch circle. Ease pastry into 9-inch pie plate; turn edges under and flute edge.

3. Combine pumpkin, remaining ⅓ cup sugar, egg whites, milk, syrup, cinnamon, ginger and remaining ½ teaspoon salt in large bowl; mix well. Pour into unbaked pie shell. Bake 15 minutes. *Reduce oven temperature to 350°F.* Continue baking 45 to 50 minutes or until center is set. Transfer to wire cooling rack; let stand at least 30 minutes before serving. Serve warm, at room temperature, or chilled with whipped topping, if desired.

makes 8 servings

NUTRIENTS PER SERVING

Calories:	226	Carbohydrate:	43g
Calories from Fat:	14%	Fiber:	2g
Total Fat:	4g	Protein:	6g
Saturated Fat:	1g	Sodium:	317mg
Cholesterol:	3mg		

Dietary Exchanges: 3 Starch, ½ Fat

Fresh Berry Pizza

Ginger Cookie Crust (recipe follows)
1½ cups fat-free ricotta cheese
3 tablespoons sugar
1 tablespoon lemon juice
2 teaspoons grated lemon peel
1 pint fresh raspberries
½ pint fresh blueberries

1. Prepare Ginger Cookie Crust; cool.

2. Combine cheese, sugar, lemon juice and lemon peel in medium bowl. Stir until smooth. Spread evenly over crust. Arrange raspberries and blueberries on top. Serve, or cover with plastic wrap and refrigerate up to 6 hours. Remove side of tart pan. Cut into 8 wedges. Garnish as desired. *makes 8 servings*

Ginger Cookie Crust

35 vanilla wafers
20 gingersnaps
1 egg white, slightly beaten

1. Preheat oven to 375°F. Combine vanilla wafers and gingersnaps in food processor; process until coarse crumbs form. Transfer to medium bowl. Stir egg white into crumbs until evenly mixed.

2. Spray 11-inch tart pan with removable bottom with nonstick cooking spray. Press crumb mixture onto bottom and up side of pan. Bake on center rack of oven 8 to 10 minutes or until firm and lightly browned. Cool in pan. *makes 1 (11-inch-diameter) crust*

NUTRIENTS PER SERVING

Calories: 272
Calories from Fat: ..23%
Total Fat: 7g
Saturated Fat: 2g
Cholesterol: 5mg
Carbohydrate: 46g
Fiber: 2g
Protein: 9g
Sodium: 225mg

Dietary Exchanges: 2 Starch, 1 Fruit, ½ Lean Meat, 1 Fat

Cocoa Molasses Bundt Cake

- 1¾ cups all-purpose flour
- 3 tablespoons unsweetened cocoa powder
- 1½ teaspoons baking powder
- 1½ teaspoons baking soda
- ½ teaspoon salt
- 1½ cups low fat buttermilk
- 1 cup granulated sugar
- ½ cup MOTT'S® Apple Sauce
- ½ cup GRANDMA'S® Molasses
- 1 whole egg
- 2 tablespoons margarine, melted
- 3 egg whites, beaten until stiff
- Powdered sugar (optional)

1. Preheat oven to 350°F. Spray 10-inch (12-cup) Bundt pan with nonstick cooking spray; flour lightly.

2. In small bowl, combine flour, cocoa, baking powder, baking soda and salt.

3. In large bowl, combine buttermilk, granulated sugar, apple sauce, molasses, whole egg and margarine.

4. Beat flour mixture into apple sauce mixture with electric mixer at low speed until moistened. Beat on high speed 3 minutes. Gently fold in beaten egg whites. Pour batter into prepared pan.

5. Bake 55 minutes or until toothpick inserted in center comes out clean. Cool on wire rack 15 minutes before removing from pan. Place cake, fluted side up, on serving plate. Cool completely. Sprinkle powdered sugar over top of cake, if desired. Cut into 12 slices.

makes 12 servings

NUTRIENTS PER SERVING

Calories:	209	Carbohydrate:	42g
Calories from Fat:	11%	Fiber:	1g
Total Fat:	3g	Protein:	4g
Saturated Fat:	1g	Sodium:	302mg
Cholesterol:	19mg		

Dietary Exchanges: 3 Starch

Rhubarb and Apple Crumble

2½ cups chopped fresh rhubarb
3 Granny Smith apples, peeled and diced
2 tablespoons cornstarch
2½ teaspoons EQUAL® FOR RECIPES *or* 8 packets EQUAL® sweetener *or* ⅓ cup EQUAL® SPOONFUL™
⅓ cup water or apple juice
1 tablespoon lemon juice
2 teaspoons finely grated lemon peel (optional)
Topping (recipe follows)

• Toss together rhubarb, apples, cornstarch and Equal®; place in 1½-quart casserole dish.

• Combine water, lemon juice and lemon peel; pour mixture over fruit. Cover and bake in preheated 400°F oven until rhubarb is tender, about 15 minutes.

• Spoon Topping evenly over fruit and bake until crisp. Serve warm with frozen lowfat yogurt or ice cream, or Vanilla Ricotta Cream (page 352), if desired.

makes 6 servings

Topping

½ cup rolled oats
¼ cup bran cereal
¼ cup raisins
¼ cup walnuts
2½ teaspoons EQUAL® FOR RECIPES *or* 8 packets EQUAL® sweetener *or* ⅓ cup EQUAL® SPOONFUL™
1 tablespoon margarine
½ to ¾ teaspoon ground cinnamon

• Place all ingredients in food processor. Pulse on and off until margarine is dispersed evenly. Or, combine all ingredients in bowl and mix with fingertips.

NUTRIENTS PER SERVING

Calories: 170	Carbohydrate: 28g
Calories from Fat: ..26%	Fiber: 5g
Total Fat: 5g	Protein: 6g
Saturated Fat: 1g	Sodium: 50mg
Cholesterol: 0mg	

Dietary Exchanges: 1 Starch, 1 Fruit, 1 Fat

Boston Cream Pie

CAKE

2¼ cups cake flour
2 teaspoons baking powder
1 teaspoon salt
½ teaspoon baking soda
1½ cups granulated sugar
2 tablespoons margarine, softened
½ cup MOTT'S® Natural Apple Sauce
½ cup skim milk
4 egg whites
1 teaspoon vanilla extract

FILLING

1 (0.9-ounce) package sugar-free instant vanilla pudding
1½ cups skim milk

CHOCOLATE GLAZE

1½ cups powdered sugar
2 tablespoons unsweetened cocoa powder
1 tablespoon skim milk
½ teaspoon vanilla extract
Lemon peel strips (optional)

1. Preheat oven to 350°F. Spray 9-inch round cake pan with nonstick cooking spray.

2. To prepare Cake, in medium bowl, combine flour, baking powder, salt and baking soda. In large bowl, beat granulated sugar and margarine with electric mixer at medium speed until blended. Whisk in apple sauce, ½ cup milk, egg whites and 1 teaspoon vanilla.

3. Add flour mixture to apple sauce mixture; stir until well blended. Pour batter into prepared pan. Bake 35 to 40 minutes or until toothpick inserted in center comes out clean. Cool completely on wire rack. Split cake horizontally in half to make 2 layers.

4. To prepare Filling, prepare pudding mix according to package directions, using 1½ cups skim milk. (Or, substitute 1½ cups prepared fat-free vanilla pudding for Filling.)

5. To prepare Chocolate Glaze, in small bowl, sift together powdered sugar and cocoa. Stir in 1 tablespoon milk and ½ teaspoon vanilla. Add water, 1 teaspoon at a time, until of desired spreading consistency. Place one cake layer on serving plate. Spread filling over cake. Top with second cake layer. Spread top of cake with Chocolate Glaze. Let stand until set. Garnish with lemon peel, if desired. Cut into 10 slices. Refrigerate leftovers. *makes 10 servings*

NUTRIENTS PER SERVING

Calories:	339	Carbohydrate:	74g
Calories from Fat:	8%	Fiber:	1g
Total Fat:	3g	Protein:	5g
Saturated Fat:	1g	Sodium:	471mg
Cholesterol:	1mg		

Dietary Exchanges: 5 Starch

Vanilla Ricotta Cream

1½ cups part-skim ricotta cheese
1 teaspoon vanilla
1 teaspoon EQUAL® FOR RECIPES *or* 3 packets EQUAL® sweetener *or* 2 tablespoons EQUAL® SPOONFUL™

• Place ricotta cheese, vanilla and Equal® in medium bowl. Beat with electric mixer until light and fluffy.

• Cover and refrigerate until ready to use.

makes 1½ cups

NUTRIENTS PER SERVING

1 tablespoon = 1 serving

Calories:	22	Carbohydrate:	1g
Calories from Fat:	50%	Fiber:	0g
Total Fat:	1g	Protein:	2g
Saturated Fat:	1g	Sodium:	19mg
Cholesterol:	5mg		

Dietary Exchanges: Free

recipe tip

Vanilla Ricotta Cream is a tasty dessert by itself. It's also a super substitute for whipped cream on scones and desserts and a terrific topping for fruit.

Apple-Cranberry Tart

1⅓ cups all-purpose flour
¾ cup plus 1 tablespoon sugar, divided
¼ teaspoon salt
2 tablespoons vegetable shortening
2 tablespoons margarine
4 to 5 tablespoons ice water
⅓ cup dried cranberries
½ cup boiling water
2 tablespoons cornstarch
1 teaspoon ground cinnamon
4 medium baking apples
Vanilla frozen yogurt (optional)

1. Combine flour, 1 tablespoon sugar and salt in medium bowl. Cut in shortening and margarine with pastry blender or two knives until mixture forms coarse crumbs. Mix in ice water, 1 tablespoon at a time, until mixture comes together and forms a soft dough. Wrap in plastic wrap. Refrigerate 30 minutes.

2. Combine cranberries and boiling water in small bowl. Let stand 20 minutes or until softened.

3. Preheat oven to 425°F. Roll out dough on floured surface to ⅛-inch thickness. Cut into 11-inch circle. Use any leftover dough scraps for decorating top of tart. Ease dough into 10-inch tart pan with removable bottom, leaving ¼ inch dough above rim. Prick bottom and sides of dough with fork. Bake 12 minutes or until dough begins to brown. Cool on wire rack. *Reduce oven temperature to 375°F.*

4. Combine remaining ¾ cup sugar and cinnamon in large bowl; mix well. Reserve 1 teaspoon mixture. Add cornstarch; mix well. Peel, core and thinly slice apples, adding pieces to bowl as they are sliced; toss well. Drain cranberries; add to apple mixture; toss well.

5. Arrange apple mixture over dough. Sprinkle reserved teaspoon sugar mixture evenly over top of tart. Place tart on baking sheet; bake 30 to 35 minutes or until apples are tender and crust is golden brown. Cool on wire rack. Remove side of pan; place tart on serving plate. Serve warm or at room temperature with frozen yogurt, if desired.

makes 8 servings

continued on page 358

Apple-Cranberry Tart, continued

NUTRIENTS PER SERVING

Calories:	263	Carbohydrate:	50g
Calories from Fat:	22%	Fiber:	2g
Total Fat:	6g	Protein:	2g
Saturated Fat:	2g	Sodium:	68mg
Cholesterol:	<1mg		

Dietary Exchanges: 1½ Starch, 1½ Fruit, 1½ Fat

Frozen Berry Ice Cream

- 8 ounces frozen unsweetened strawberries, partially thawed
- 8 ounces frozen unsweetened peaches, partially thawed
- 4 ounces frozen unsweetened blueberries, partially thawed
- 6 packets sugar substitute
- 2 teaspoons vanilla
- 2 cups no-sugar-added light vanilla ice cream
- 16 blueberries
- 4 small strawberries, halved
- 8 peach slices

1. In food processor, combine frozen strawberries, peaches, blueberries, sugar substitute and vanilla. Process until coarsely chopped.

2. Add ice cream; process until well blended.

3. Serve immediately for semi-soft texture, or freeze until needed and allow to stand 10 minutes before serving to soften slightly. *makes 8 servings*

NUTRIENTS PER SERVING

½ cup = 1 serving

Calories:	69	Carbohydrate:	15g
Calories from Fat:	2%	Fiber:	1g
Total Fat:	<1g	Protein:	3g
Saturated Fat:	<1g	Sodium:	23mg
Cholesterol:	0mg		

Dietary Exchanges: 1 Starch

Low Fat Devil's Chocolate Fudge Cake

1 cup water
½ cup Dried Plum Purée (recipe follows) or prepared dried plum butter
3 egg whites
1½ teaspoons vanilla
1 cup plus 2 tablespoons all-purpose flour
1 cup plus 2 tablespoons granulated sugar
¾ cup unsweetened cocoa powder
1½ teaspoons baking powder
¼ teaspoon baking soda
¼ teaspoon salt

Preheat oven to 350°F. Coat 9-inch square baking pan with vegetable cooking spray. To make cake, in mixer bowl, beat water, dried plum purée, egg whites and vanilla until well blended. Add flour, granulated sugar, ¾ cup cocoa, baking powder, baking soda and salt; mix well. Spread batter evenly in prepared pan. Bake in center of oven about 30 minutes until pick inserted into center comes out clean. Cool completely in pan on wire rack.

makes 9 servings

Dried Plum Purée: Combine 1⅓ cups (8 ounces) pitted dried plums and 6 tablespoons hot water in container of food processor or blender. Pulse on and off until dried plums are finely chopped and smooth. Store leftovers in a covered container in the refrigerator for up to two months.

Favorite recipe from **California Dried Plum Board**

NUTRIENTS PER SERVING

Calories: 229
Calories from Fat: ..1%
Total Fat: ....<1g
Saturated Fat: .....<1g
Cholesterol: ......<1mg
Carbohydrate: 54g
Fiber: 2g
Protein: 4g
Sodium: 213mg

Dietary Exchanges: 2½ Starch, 1 Fruit

Lemon Raspberry Tiramisu

- 2 packages (8 ounces each) fat-free cream cheese, softened
- 6 packages artificial sweetener *or* equivalent of ¼ cup sugar
- 1 teaspoon vanilla
- ⅓ cup water
- 1 package (0.3 ounce) sugar-free lemon-flavored gelatin
- 2 cups thawed frozen fat-free nondairy whipped topping
- ½ cup all-fruit red raspberry preserves
- ¼ cup water
- 2 tablespoons marsala wine
- 2 packages (3 ounces each) ladyfingers
- 1 pint fresh raspberries or frozen unsweetened raspberries, thawed

1. Combine cream cheese, artificial sweetener and vanilla in large bowl. Beat with electric mixer at high speed until smooth; set aside.

2. Combine water and gelatin in small microwavable bowl; microwave at HIGH 30 seconds to 1 minute or until water is boiling and gelatin is dissolved. Cool slightly.

3. Add gelatin mixture to cheese mixture; beat 1 minute. Add whipped topping; beat 1 minute more, scraping side of bowl. Set aside.

4. Whisk together preserves, water and marsala in small bowl until well blended. Reserve 2 tablespoons of preserves mixture; set aside. Spread ⅓ cup preserves mixture evenly over bottom of 11×7-inch glass baking dish.

5. Split ladyfingers in half; place half in bottom of baking dish. Spread half of cheese mixture evenly over ladyfingers; sprinkle 1 cup of raspberries evenly over cheese mixture. Top with remaining ladyfingers; spread remaining preserves mixture over ladyfingers. Top with remaining cheese mixture. Cover; refrigerate for at least 2 hours. Sprinkle with remaining raspberries and drizzle with reserved 2 tablespoons of preserves mixture before serving.

makes 12 servings

NUTRIENTS PER SERVING

Calories:	158	Carbohydrate:	26g
Calories from Fat:	9%	Fiber:	1g
Total Fat:	1g	Protein:	7g
Saturated Fat:	<1g	Sodium:	272mg
Cholesterol:	52mg		

Dietary Exchanges: 2 Starch

Frozen Sundae Pie

26 chocolate wafer cookies
4 cups fat-free ice cream, slightly softened
2 tablespoons fat-free hot fudge ice cream topping
1 cup banana slices
2 tablespoons fat-free caramel ice cream topping
1 ounce reduced-fat dry roasted peanuts, crushed

1. Place cookies on bottom and around side of 9-inch pie pan. Carefully spoon ice cream into pie pan; cover with plastic wrap. Freeze 2 hours or overnight or until firm.

2. Just before serving, place fudge topping in small microwavable bowl; microwave at HIGH 10 seconds. Drizzle pie with fudge topping; top with banana slices. Place caramel topping in small microwavable bowl; microwave at HIGH 10 seconds. Drizzle over bananas; sprinkle with peanuts. *makes 8 servings*

note: If desired, the pie may be assembled the night before without the bananas. Top pie with bananas at time of serving.

NUTRIENTS PER SERVING

Calories:	252	Carbohydrate:	49g
Calories from Fat:	17%	Fiber:	1g
Total Fat:	5g	Protein:	7g
Saturated Fat:	1g	Sodium:	210mg
Cholesterol:	<1mg		

Dietary Exchanges: 3 Starch, 1 Fat

Everyone's sure to enjoy this cool and creamy dessert on hot summer days. You'll especially appreciate it because not only is it easy to make, it doesn't require baking. So, you don't have to endure the extra heat from the oven.

JELL-O® 'n Juice Parfaits

- 2 cups boiling water, divided
- 1 package (4-serving size) JELL-O® Brand Strawberry Flavor Sugar Free Low Calorie Gelatin
- 1 package (4-serving size) JELL-O® Brand Lemon Flavor Sugar Free Low Calorie Gelatin
- 2 cups cold apple juice, divided
- 1 tub (8 ounces) COOL WHIP FREE® Whipped Topping, thawed

STIR 1 cup boiling water into each of the strawberry and lemon gelatins in separate bowls at least 2 minutes until completely dissolved. Stir 1 cup apple juice into each bowl. Pour into separate 9-inch square pans.

REFRIGERATE 4 hours or until firm. Cut gelatin in each pan into ½-inch cubes. Layer alternating flavors of gelatin and whipped topping in 8 dessert glasses. Garnish with additional whipped topping, if desired.

makes 8 servings

Prep: 10 minutes plus refrigerating

NUTRIENTS PER SERVING

Calories:	85	Carbohydrate:	17g
Calories from Fat:	1%	Fiber:	<1g
Total Fat:	<1g	Protein:	1g
Saturated Fat:	<1g	Sodium:	67mg
Cholesterol:	0mg		

Dietary Exchanges: 1 Starch

"Parfait" is the French word for "perfect." Layered in tall, footed, clear glasses known as parfait glasses, the traditional French version of this dish is made with egg yolks, sugar, whipped cream and flavoring. JELL-O® 'n Juice Parfaits are a fresh and light twist on this classic dessert.

Double Layer Chocolate Fudge Pie

- 2 cups cold fat free milk, divided
- 1 package (4-serving size) JELL-O® Chocolate Fudge or Chocolate Flavor Fat Free Sugar Free Instant Reduced Calorie Pudding & Pie Filling
- 1 tub (8 ounces) COOL WHIP LITE Whipped Topping, thawed, divided
- 1 prepared reduced fat graham cracker crumb crust (6 ounces or 9 inches)*
- 1 package (4-serving size) JELL-O® White Chocolate or Vanilla Flavor Fat Free Sugar Free Instant Reduced Calorie Pudding & Pie Filling

**Nutritionals reflect regular (not reduced-fat) graham cracker crumb crust.*

POUR 1 cup milk into medium bowl. Add chocolate fudge flavor pudding mix. Beat with wire whisk 1 minute. (Mixture will be thick.) Gently stir in ½ of the whipped topping. Spoon evenly into crust.

POUR remaining 1 cup milk into another medium bowl. Add white chocolate flavor pudding mix. Beat with wire whisk 1 minute. (Mixture will be thick.) Gently stir in remaining whipped topping (1½ cups). Spread over pudding layer in crust.

REFRIGERATE 4 hours or until set. Garnish with additional whipped topping, if desired. *makes 8 servings*

Prep Time: 10 minutes
Refrigerate Time: 4 hours

NUTRIENTS PER SERVING
(without additional garnish)

Calories:	229	Carbohydrate:	30g
Calories from Fat:	38%	Fiber:	1g
Total Fat:	9g	Protein:	4g
Saturated Fat:	5g	Sodium:	330mg
Cholesterol:	1mg		

Dietary Exchanges: 2 Starch, 2 Fat

Blackberry Strudel Cups

- 6 sheets frozen phyllo dough, thawed
- Nonstick cooking spray
- 1 pint blackberries
- 2 tablespoons sugar
- 1 cup thawed frozen reduced-fat nondairy whipped topping
- 1 container (6 ounces) custard-style apricot or peach low-fat yogurt
- Mint sprigs for garnish

Preheat oven to 400°F. Cut phyllo dough crosswise into 4 pieces. Coat 1 piece lightly with cooking spray; place in large custard cup. Coat remaining 3 pieces lightly with cooking spray; place over first piece, alternating corners. Repeat with remaining phyllo dough to form 6 strudel cups. Place custard cups on cookie sheet; bake about 15 minutes or until pastry is golden. Let cool to room temperature.

Meanwhile, combine blackberries and sugar in small bowl; let stand 15 minutes. Mix whipped topping and yogurt in medium bowl. Reserve ½ cup blackberries for garnish; gently stir remaining blackberries into whipped topping mixture. Spoon into cooled pastry cups. Garnish with reserved blackberries and mint sprigs.

makes 6 servings

NUTRIENTS PER SERVING

Calories:	125	Carbohydrate:	25g
Calories from Fat:	22%	Fiber:	3g
Total Fat:	4g	Protein:	3g
Saturated Fat:	<1g	Sodium:	22mg
Cholesterol:	3mg		

Dietary Exchanges: 1½ Fruit, 1 Fat

Blackberry Strudel Cup

Turtle Cheesecake

- 6 tablespoons reduced-fat margarine
- 1½ cups graham cracker crumbs
- 2 envelopes unflavored gelatin
- ½ cup cold water
- 2 containers (8 ounces each) fat-free cream cheese
- 2 cups 1% low-fat cottage cheese
- 1 cup sugar
- 1½ teaspoons vanilla
- 1 container (8 ounces) reduced-fat nondairy whipped topping, thawed
- ¼ cup prepared fat-free caramel topping
- ¼ cup prepared fat-free hot fudge topping
- ¼ cup chopped pecans

1. Spray bottom and side of 9-inch springform pan with nonstick cooking spray. Preheat oven to 350°F. Melt margarine in small saucepan over medium heat. Stir in graham cracker crumbs. Press crumb mixture firmly onto side or bottom of prepared pan. Bake 10 minutes. Cool.

2. Sprinkle gelatin over water in small saucepan. Let stand 3 minutes to soften. Heat gelatin mixture over low heat until completely dissolved, stirring constantly.

3. Combine cream cheese, cottage cheese, sugar and vanilla in food processor or blender; process until smooth. Add gelatin mixture; process until well blended. Fold in whipped topping. Pour into prepared crust. Refrigerate 4 hours or until set.

4. Loosen cake from rim of pan. Remove side of pan from cake. Drizzle caramel and hot fudge toppings over cheesecake. Sprinkle pecans evenly over top of cake before serving. *makes 16 servings*

NUTRIENTS PER SERVING

Calories:	232	Carbohydrate:	32g
Calories from Fat:	26%	Fiber:	<1g
Total Fat:	7g	Protein:	10g
Saturated Fat:	1g	Sodium:	444mg
Cholesterol:	5mg		

Dietary Exchanges: 2 Starch, ½ Lean Meat, 1 Fat

Mocha Pudding Parfaits

1½ cups cold fat free milk
1 tablespoon MAXWELL HOUSE® Instant Coffee
1 package (4-serving size) JELL-O® Chocolate Flavor Fat Free Sugar Free Instant Reduced Calorie Pudding & Pie Filling
1 tub (8 ounces) COOL WHIP FREE® Whipped Topping, thawed, divided
6 reduced fat chocolate wafer cookies, chopped

POUR milk and coffee into medium bowl. Add pudding mix. Beat with wire whisk 1 minute. Gently stir in ½ of the whipped topping.

SPOON ½ of the pudding mixture evenly into 6 dessert dishes. Sprinkle with chopped cookies. Top with ½ of the remaining whipped topping. Top with remaining pudding mixture. Garnish each serving with a spoonful of remaining whipped topping.

REFRIGERATE until ready to serve. *makes 6 servings*

great substitute: The coffee can be omitted. Drizzle each serving with 1 teaspoon fat free chocolate syrup for a really indulgent treat! (Nutrition will vary.)

Prep Time: 10 minutes

NUTRIENTS PER SERVING

1 parfait = 1 serving

Calories:	126	Carbohydrate:	24g
Calories from Fat:	9%	Fiber:	<1g
Total Fat:	1g	Protein:	3g
Saturated Fat:	<1g	Sodium:	260mg
Cholesterol:	1mg		

Dietary Exchanges: 1½ Starch

Peach and Plum Cobbler

- 2½ cups thinly sliced unpeeled plums
- 2 cups thinly sliced peeled peaches*
- 2 tablespoons frozen pineapple juice concentrate
- 1 tablespoon peach brandy or orange liqueur
- ⅛ teaspoon ground cardamom
- 1¼ cups plus 2 tablespoons all-purpose flour, divided
- 1½ teaspoons baking powder
- ¼ teaspoon salt
- 2 teaspoons sugar, divided
- 1 ounce cold reduced-fat cream cheese, cut into 6 pieces
- 1 tablespoon cold butter, cut into 6 pieces
- ¼ cup low-fat (1%) milk, divided
- 1 egg
- Fat-free ice cream (optional)

**To loosen peach skins for easy peeling, plunge peaches into boiling water for 30 seconds, then into cold water.*

1. Preheat oven to 425°F. Spray 8-inch glass baking dish with nonstick cooking spray.

2. Combine plums, peaches, pineapple juice, peach brandy, cardamom and 2 tablespoons flour in medium bowl; toss gently. Spoon into prepared baking dish.

3. Combine remaining 1¼ cups flour, baking powder, salt and 1¾ teaspoons sugar in medium bowl; mix well. Using pastry blender or two knives cut cream cheese and butter into flour mixture until mixture resembles coarse crumbs. Set aside.

4. Reserve 1 teaspoon milk for glaze. Beat remaining milk and egg in small bowl. Pour all at once into flour mixture; stir quickly with fork until just moistened. Gather dough into a ball; place on lightly floured board.

5. If dough is sticky, sprinkle with additional flour; knead 12 times. Roll dough into 8-inch square, about ¾ inch thick.

6. Place dough over top of fruit, pressing down around fruit at edges. Brush dough with reserved 1 teaspoon milk; sprinkle with remaining ¼ teaspoon sugar. Bake about 30 minutes or until top is lightly browned and fruit is tender. Serve warm topped with ice cream, if desired.

makes 6 servings

NUTRIENTS PER SERVING

Calories:	265	Carbohydrate:	50g
Calories from Fat:	16%	Fiber:	3g
Total Fat:	5g	Protein:	6g
Saturated Fat:	2g	Sodium:	279mg
Cholesterol:	43mg		

Dietary Exchanges: 1½ Starch, 2 Fruit, ½ Fat

Key Lime Cheesecake with Strawberries and Fresh Mint

12 whole low-fat honey graham crackers, broken into small pieces
2 tablespoons reduced-fat margarine
2 packages (8 ounces each) reduced-fat cream cheese
1 package (8 ounces) nonfat cream cheese
1 container (8 ounces) plain nonfat yogurt
⅔ cup powdered sugar
¼ cup lime juice
8 packets sugar substitute *or* equivalent of ⅓ cup sugar, divided
2 teaspoons lime peel
1½ teaspoons vanilla
3 cups fresh strawberries, quartered
2 tablespoons finely chopped mint leaves

1. Preheat oven to 350°F. Coat 9-inch springform baking pan with nonstick cooking spray; set aside.

2. Place graham cracker pieces and margarine in food processor or blender; pulse until coarse in texture. Gently press crumb mixture onto bottom and up ½ inch side of pan. Bake 8 to 10 minutes or until lightly browned; cool completely on wire rack.

3. Beat cream cheese, yogurt, powdered sugar, lime juice, 6 packets sugar substitute, lime peel and vanilla in large bowl with electric mixer at high speed until smooth. Pour into cooled pie crust. Cover with plastic wrap; freeze 2 hours or refrigerate overnight.

4. Combine strawberries, remaining 2 packets sugar substitute and mint in medium bowl 30 minutes before serving; set aside. Just before serving, spoon strawberry mixture over cheesecake. *makes 12 servings*

NUTRIENTS PER SERVING

Calories:	176	Carbohydrate:	18g
Calories from Fat:	35%	Fiber:	1g
Total Fat:	7g	Protein:	8g
Saturated Fat:	5g	Sodium:	341mg
Cholesterol:	20mg		

Dietary Exchanges: 1 Starch, 1 Lean Meat, 1 Fat

The publisher would like to thank the companies and organizations listed below for the use of their recipes and photographs in this publication.

A.1.® Steak Sauce

Birds Eye®

Butterball® Turkey Company

California Dried Plum Board

California Poultry Federation

California Tree Fruit Agreement

ConAgra Grocery Products Company

Cream of Wheat® Cereal

Del Monte Corporation

Dole Food Company, Inc.

Egg Beaters®

Equal® sweetener

Filippo Berio® Olive Oil

Florida Department of Agriculture and Consumer Services, Bureau of Seafood and Aquaculture

General Mills, Inc.

Hershey Foods Corporation

Kellogg Company

Kraft Foods Holdings

Michigan Apple Committee

Minnesota Cultivated Wild Rice Council

Mott's® is a registered trademark of Mott's, Inc.

National Honey Board

National Turkey Federation

Peanut Advisory Board

The Quaker® Oatmeal Kitchens

Reckitt Benckiser

Sargento® Foods Inc.

The Sugar Association, Inc.

Sunkist Growers

Unilever Bestfoods North America

USA Rice Federation

Washington Apple Commission

Wisconsin Milk Marketing Board

C

T

METRIC CONVERSION CHART

VOLUME MEASUREMENTS (dry)

$1/8$ teaspoon = 0.5 mL
$1/4$ teaspoon = 1 mL
$1/2$ teaspoon = 2 mL
$3/4$ teaspoon = 4 mL
1 teaspoon = 5 mL
1 tablespoon = 15 mL
2 tablespoons = 30 mL
$1/4$ cup = 60 mL
$1/3$ cup = 75 mL
$1/2$ cup = 125 mL
$2/3$ cup = 150 mL
$3/4$ cup = 175 mL
1 cup = 250 mL
2 cups = 1 pint = 500 mL
3 cups = 750 mL
4 cups = 1 quart = 1 L

VOLUME MEASUREMENTS (fluid)

1 fluid ounce (2 tablespoons) = 30 mL
4 fluid ounces ($1/2$ cup) = 125 mL
8 fluid ounces (1 cup) = 250 mL
12 fluid ounces ($1\,1/2$ cups) = 375 mL
16 fluid ounces (2 cups) = 500 mL

WEIGHTS (mass)

$1/2$ ounce = 15 g
1 ounce = 30 g
3 ounces = 90 g
4 ounces = 120 g
8 ounces = 225 g
10 ounces = 285 g
12 ounces = 360 g
16 ounces = 1 pound = 450 g

DIMENSIONS

$1/16$ inch = 2 mm
$1/8$ inch = 3 mm
$1/4$ inch = 6 mm
$1/2$ inch = 1.5 cm
$3/4$ inch = 2 cm
1 inch = 2.5 cm

OVEN TEMPERATURES

250°F = 120°C
275°F = 140°C
300°F = 150°C
325°F = 160°C
350°F = 180°C
375°F = 190°C
400°F = 200°C
425°F = 220°C
450°F = 230°C

BAKING PAN SIZES

Utensil	Size in Inches/Quarts	Metric Volume	Size in Centimeters
Baking or Cake Pan (square or rectangular)	8×8×2	2 L	20×20×5
	9×9×2	2.5 L	23×23×5
	12×8×2	3 L	30×20×5
	13×9×2	3.5 L	33×23×5
Loaf Pan	8×4×3	1.5 L	20×10×7
	9×5×3	2 L	23×13×7
Round Layer Cake Pan	8×1½	1.2 L	20×4
	9×1½	1.5 L	23×4
Pie Plate	8×1¼	750 mL	20×3
	9×1¼	1 L	23×3
Baking Dish or Casserole	1 quart	1 L	—
	1½ quart	1.5 L	—
	2 quart	2 L	—